May
you always
know the
light you
are!

Blessings
Jane

I'll Take God

–

Hold the Religion

-A Memoir-

by irene M. Tomkinson, MSW

authorHOUSE®

AuthorHouse™
1663 Liberty Drive
Bloomington, IN 47403
www.authorhouse.com
Phone: 1 (800) 839-8640

Published by AuthorHouse 01/13/2018

ISBN: 978-1-5462-2189-0 (sc)
ISBN: 978-1-5462-2260-6 (e)

Print information available on the last page.

Contents

What folks are saying about I'll Take God-Hold the Religion

"Picture a loving grandmother, meets samurai warrior, meets stand-up comic; that is Irene Tomkinson. Sharing with us her brave wisdom, fierce compassion and incredible heart, she unfolds her life story in an easy and engaging way. You start to understand the threads of meaning in your own life, seeing your own struggles and successes through new eyes. *I'll Take God-Hold the Religion* will make you laugh out loud, cry from the deep, and cheer for joy...and you will love it!"
Uma Maeke Abrami, Voice Teacher and Coach

"I love *I'll Take God-Hold the Religion*. Irene helps us to see that God is much more than we were ever taught to believe. Through her questions, exercises and sharing her experiences, she helps us uncover our false beliefs about ourselves so that we can remember that God's loves is us."
Bonnie Kimball, Camera Operator

"Author Irene Tomkinson makes no bones about her view of religion, but don't let the title fool you, this is a raw, deftly written story about life and not losing faith no matter what bucket of lemons you have been handed. With gritty authenticity and compelling story telling, Irene takes the reader on a grace-filled journey through the tender crevices of her difficult yet faith-filled life. *I'll Take God – Hold the Religion* has something for everyone: love, loss, triumph, self-discovery and yes, God's constant presence through it all." **Kelly T. Hurley, Founder of Faith to Flourish & 8000 Voices**

"This is one fine soul polisher! *I'll Take God-Hold the Religion* is magnificent. Of course it is. It's from her guts, and that's where I think God really lives. See Genesis 32:22-32." *Sam Deibler, M.Div., Community Organizer & Biblical Scholar*

"I'll Take God – Hold the Religion is an entertaining, yet poignant trip through the religious and spiritual development of a gifted writer and therapist. Tomkinson's story is a compact jewel which will move you to tears, laughter and deeply personal growth."
Dr. Everett Moitoza, Consulting Psychologist

"I'll Take God – Hold the Religion is more than a memoir. While Irene authentically shares the ups and downs of her life's journey, she also invites us to join her through questions found at the end of each chapter. You see, she has this knack – a KNOWING – for asking questions or making comments that precisely cut through the "thickness of life" down to that which is more essential. These questions are as "on point" as the ones I have experienced during even our most casual conversations. Whether you explore the questions or not, I can unequivocally say there is something

in this book for you. You may see differently and even re-make yourself better than before. Whatever it is, this book is worth the read." **Rev. Dr. Paul Hasselbeck, Author and Speaker**

"As a nurse and a woman in recovery I recommend *I'll Take God – Hold the Religion* as a must read for all. I too grew up in a religion that I came to resent. Irene's book led me to realize that there is a Being greater than us. Her book helped heal a part of my past that I hope to bring into my career as a nurse. People touch lives in many different capacities. This book touched my life greatly. Learning to surrender to a power greater than ourselves can be a difficult action. This book showed me it doesn't have to be impossible. By believing in a power greater than myself, I can pull strength from that power to stay clean and to provide compassionate care to my patients. Irene's wisdom is life- changing for me. I hope to draw upon her strength to change the life of the patients I am privileged to care for." *Tammy D, RN in recovery*

"I'll Take GOD - Hold the Religion spoke deeply to my heart and soul, Tomkinson knows how to steer you toward your inner Self with her 5 Cairns to keep you spiritually on track. Her honesty with the reader is brilliant and very welcoming. No sugar coating, just compelling honesty about how life carries you on your journey. Grab yourself a journal and cup of tea, and get down with your inner Truth and Love. Love really is the answer to all of our questions." **Rebecca Johnson, Member of IBEW LOCAL 1837 - NH**

"I loved reading *I'll Take God – Hold the Religion* even better the second time! Tomkinson's writing is refreshingly honest and clear, particularly when it comes to the complicated subject of God. Regardless of one's upbringing, there is something for everyone in this story that speaks to the heart. It spoke to mine." **Denise Day, Children's Advocate and Elected School Board member**

"I have been blessed! I've just finished *I'll Take God- Hold the Religion.* I am wrapped up in layers of appreciation, awe and peace. This book has a flavor bigger than just the words on paper, bigger than each chapter, bigger, even than the cairns the author describes so beautifully. The bigger flavor for me is LOVE. Tomkinson is human, no doubt about it, flesh and blood like you and me. She weaves a part of herself into this story that feels like it bridges the pages and holds my hands as I see and discover myself . . . safely. I see my story in her experience. This author is relatable. Her book reads like Hope. Hope and Love." Diana **Tuano, Special Needs Educator**

"Tomkinson has written an irreverent page-turner that will first make you cry, then laugh, then propel you to the core of your soul. *I'll Take God – Hold the Religion* is for anyone of any religion or no religion, whose dogma has failed them. Through her very personal story she ignites a bomb in the faith conversation, and then shows you the way back to your truth." **Karen Fitzgerald, Life Coach, Actress, Writer**

"Irene is a very dear friend, confidant, gifted therapist and way-shower to me. This is how she presents herself in her new book, *I'll Take God – Hold the Religion.* She exposes her whole life for all to see and uses it to show us how to find our Inner- Self, Soul, Being, Peace. Each chapter culminates with a list of questions. My suggestion would be to take them seriously, as I have. I can't tell you how many times, as my hand poised at the doorknob to leave after a conversation with Irene, she would suggest a question for my inner child which would occupy my mind for days -always perfect of course. I felt this same level of comfort as I read the book. Irene, being very intuitive, has a Knowingness that is beyond compare. This book is for you. Trust me, the questions are the best part. I love this book and look forward to more. No pressure Irene!" **Al Austgen, Airline Pilot and "Light of the World"**

"I love *I'll Take God- Hold the Religion*. Tomkinson's writing kept me wanting to read more, and the content is so relevant and important...What more can I say!" *Ann Shifman-Deibler, IT Consultant and Web Contractor*

"I just finished *I'll Take God – Hold the Religion*. I was amazed how quickly I read it. Then I realized that it wasn't that quick. It was that I couldn't put it down and read right through it. There were many "a-ha" moments. This story can't help but reach every reader in some thought-provoking way. It is not about religion but rather a life experience that so many of us share ... beautifully written." *Lorna Ruth, MA, Lic. Life Coach, Certified Mediator*

"I'll Take God – Hold the Religion is going to help so many people, especially those in recovery who are ready to claim who they are as God's Child. This is one of those books I will be giving to everyone I love. I like the humor.

I identified with the story. I became absorbed by the book. Today I picked up chapter 16 and it dug into me till I was finished with it. I was surprised how much I related. This doesn't happen very often with me, and I read almost everything." **Arthur Gay, Teacher of A Course in Miracles**

"Irene Tomkinson's brave and transparent telling of the spiritual milestones and turning points in her life was a validation for me. As a child and young adult, I lived under the well-intentioned yet insidious violation of my soul's authenticity in the church of my family. *I'll Take God-Hold the Religion* is a mentoring and brave voice in the void. I found someone who knew where I had been and found a way out. This book offered light on my path. I am blessed to have read it and you will be too." **Dr. David Farnsworth, PsyD**

"I loved this book because it resonated for me on many levels. I have struggled with church and religion since I was small. I hated the word God. I was taught about a punishing God. I grew up with a lot of shame and guilt, feelings of worthlessness. Twenty-nine years ago, when I joined AA I had to find my own higher power. I discovered one that I felt truly loved me and saved me. I am grateful to have read this story and know that Irene felt the same as me. I think this book will help so many women who have dealt with the same feelings of guilt and shame. It is truly inspirational, and I'm blessed to have read it. I fully connected to it on a spiritual and emotional level. Others will benefit as well. Reading *I'll Take God-Hold the Religion* was a gift." **Laura Powers, Active Recovery Sponsor**

I'll
Take
God
-
Hold
The
Religion

Acknowledgments

To date I have written two books. For me, the writing process takes more than a village. My process needs an army of friends, family, and strangers. I have been showered with support way beyond what is fair or reasonable for any one human being to be blessed. I want great big huge words to convey my gratitude. I need words that can paint the complete picture of my overflowing heart. Words that show the depth of my awe and wonder for the richness of my human community. I come down to two...Thank You.

To my over-talented -underpaid staff –

David Tomkinson - Dee, how can I ever thank you enough? You have gifted me with more patience than is earthly possible. Who knew how all your English classes at Syracuse would pay off for me?

Shawn Tomkinson - It is magical to have a professional photographer in the family. You make everyone look so good. Thank you

Brian Doser (the Music Man) Thank you for the wonderful recording sessions. We both know I had no idea what I was doing. Thank goodness you did.

Katie Sarno - You are the best production assistant anyone could ask for.

Trice Atkinson - Thank you for uncomplicating the complicated world of tech for me.

Uma Maeke - Thank you for the big Go Ahead. You gave me that wonderful push off the high dive. Thank you, coach.

Jackie Watson- Thank you for your wonderful creative eye and over-the-top loyal support. I love that I know you, a famous animator.

Karen Fitzgerald – Thank you for being there for Carrie and being there for me.

Susan Luddy – Thank you for your continued loyalty, support and generous heart.

Earth Angels

Dr. Steven Smith, Dr. Everett Moitoza, Elizabeth Moitoza, Lisa Natoli, Bill Free, Kelly Hurley, Laura Powers, Arthur Gay, Rebecca Johnson, Bonnie Kimball, Judy Batchelder, Denise Day, Karen Gormley, Diana Tuano, Beverly Rollins, Holly Morency Gleason, Marisa Jarvis, Lorna Felt, Kate Portrie, Rev. Dr. Paul Hasselbeck, Geoff Farnsworth, Dot Farnsworth, Terri Clements, Jackie Watson, Nancy Aronie, Sam Diebler, Tammy Druesendahl, Etta Sears, Al Augsten, Brian Dosier, David Roth, Diane Morrison, Diana Ma Johnson, Jill Hibyan, Amy Wheeler, Kristina George, Dr. Rhonda Karg, Ann Shifman-Deibler, Dr. Toni Manougran, Scott Pare, Lynn Morell…

And always *Julia Morell,* the world's best granddaughter… because you like that your Mammy puts your name in her books.

Dedication

This work is dedicated to my two favorite "old men."

To my step-dad, John J. Davey (1923-2017)
Dad, ever since I was 22 when you married mom,
you had my back. I miss you every day.

To my husband of 47 years, David S. Tomkinson
You have always believed in me till I could believe in myself...
there is no greater gift.

Together you both raised me up, so I can stand on mountains.

Love
This

Introduction

At twenty-one, I stomped away from the Catholic Church and God. To me they were one and the same and I was done with both. I no longer believed either could be trusted. From that point on every time I said God I choked. I had given God (as taught by my religion) my faith and trust, and for that I believed I was betrayed. No, mine is not a story of being sexually abused by a priest. I felt betrayed by my own innocence and naiveté. I was sabotaged by myself. I didn't pay attention to my gut. And I paid a big price. Can you relate? How often have you not listened to your KNOWING?

And how did that work out for you?

At 61 while riding my bike across a small bridge in Cortez, Florida, I was thanking the "Universe" for the beauty surrounding me. In that moment I realized how much I had changed. I had become a woman who called herself spiritual but not religious. I was continually filled with gratitude to Something. What was the Something and what did I mean by spiritual? I knew what I didn't believe or accept about God. But what did I believe?

Okay, so as I rode across the bridge I kept hearing the words "when I say God I choke." I remember wondering if those words were a title for my next book. I made note and then moved on to whatever my brain played with next. But the words got hung up on some lobe. For days they rustled like a tangled kite stuck in a branch. Eventually, I climbed the tree and saved the kite. I laid it out on my desk. Under the light of scrutiny, the questions started. Those words were the impetus that motivated me to write this book. It was not until I was almost finished that I realized the title had to be I'LL TAKE GOD–HOLD THE RELIGION.

Once I heard an author (whose name I can't remember) being interviewed on NPR say, "Writers don't write because they have the answers. They write because they have the questions." She was right on for me. I had changed from a child who loved the church and God, to a woman whose head swirled in snarky remarks whenever I had to attend a Catholic wedding. I clenched my teeth whenever anyone used the "G" word or any of his nicknames such as the Divine, Higher Power or The Almighty Whatever. And now I am a woman who is consistently giving thanks to the Great Something. What changed? What happened?

As a child I loved the Church. I loved it with the unconditional love that only a child and dog can give. I listened to the ordained ones and followed the rules. I did everything the priests and nuns told me. I was instructed to trust their authority. I followed the rules right off the cliff of that trust.

Stunned when I hit bottom, I believed I had been betrayed by my innocence, youth, and naiveté, by my love and faith. This perceived betrayal forged an internal split that separated me from my core. Today I believe that core is my connection to God. It took twenty years of searching and seeking to find my way back.

The odyssey back to God led me through marriages, religions, births and deaths, alcohol, cigarettes, sex, and rock and roll. It often pulled me by my hair kicking and screaming. Sometimes the journey could be gentle and kind, holding me with the warmth of a hot bubble bath. Then on a whim, it would turn vicious like an ocean storm.

This is my story of recognizing how I had let others define God for me. My religious training taught me that God was an outside force. One who was to be obeyed and feared. I had no skills or references for how to separate God and the Church. I didn't know they were not one and the same. To me they were like an old married couple; I could not see them as individuals.

Eventually, often with my fists clamped tight, I found the God of my understanding. You see, I never lost my belief in a greater Presence. I believed alright...I believed *He* couldn't be trusted! He pissed me off, and at the same time, I was stuck because I needed *Him*. Paradoxically, I wanted my children to have God. I wanted them to have a sense of Something larger than themselves. At the time I didn't know the difference between religion and spirituality. I was only sure about one thing...I was *not* going to raise them in the Catholic Church. This resolve scared me. I was fine with challenging the old rules for myself. But to not have the girls raised in the "one true Church" scared me. Was I risking God's wrath on their beautiful little souls? Did I mention the guilt storm (which was my normal weather pattern) because of my mother's disappointment with my choices?

To walk (more like stomp) away from my mother's church

was frightening. Visions of my girls damned to eternal hell because I was not raising them Catholic haunted me. The cogent part of my intellect could not get the indoctrinated voice in my brain to knock off the old superstitious clamor. My old childhood God, of judgment and rules, was buried deep in my psyche. I had to walk through the anxiety and guilt. Irrational terror had me doomed to some really-nasty punishment for not obeying the rules.

Covered in mud and slugs, soaking wet, I did make it out of the swamp and ultimately better for the wear. The journey to my new God took me on a wild ride. At the time I didn't know the trip would deliver me to myself. It would have been a lot easier if I had learned these lessons sooner.

Old beliefs and old rules jammed my progress over and over again. Years ago, before I left the Church, I remember hearing a priest pitching to young parents to reassure them and convince them to bring their kids to catechism classes. His words went something like, "If the Church can have your children to educate before seven, you parents can be assured the Church will have them for life." There was a lot of truth in that statement. Undoing my childhood programming has been a long and arduous journey.

Often, we get angry–we don't get clear. Anger locks things in place. It gives us self-righteousness to chew on like gum that has lost its flavor. Why would you want your childhood programming to be examined? Here's why: Without awareness we are being pushed around by old beliefs and ideas that may not fit us anymore. These beliefs are defaults making choices for us without our permission. They are ingrained in our psyche from such a young age that we react as if they are a law like gravity, rather than a learned response. To be conscious, we need to inventory our beliefs, recognize where they originated and ask ourselves if they still fit. Or do they belong to someone else, and are we blindly carrying them?

I want to save you some steps, to save you some time. I want to offer my experience, strength, and hope. Like many older people, I want to spare you pain and dead-end paths. I long for you to discover what's in *your* heart so that you may learn to honor your TRUTH with confidence and freedom. To KNOW with a capital K the truth that is yours. I want you to be able to hold on to your truth when the outside world, including family, can be filling you with fear and doubt. By sharing my journey, I pray to help you with yours.

Along the way, I have used five life-affirming practices. I struggled to find the right word to label them. Nothing fit until one morning while having breakfast with my good friend Everett, I shared I was looking for a word that described guidance or a lighted path. I didn't want a word that smelled like dogma. (Pun intended.)

He suggested the word *cairn* (pronounced two ways... like the name Karen or carn). You know, those piles of rocks that other hikers have left on trails to mark the path? They don't tell you which way to go. They just let you know you are on the right path. That was it. It resonated in the middle of my solar plexus. I love cairns. They are a comfort for any hiker on any trail. Fellow travelers lay them on the trail, and each of us can add a rock to help the next person in line. They are gentle, and they are made of natural materials. They are an international symbol. You don't need them to be interpreted.

Throughout my story, it will become obvious when I did

and did not have cairns on my path. The five cairns I will share with you throughout the book will guide you on your way. Most likely, you are using some of them already. My goal is to make you conscious of your use and to encourage you to trust what you KNOW. The guide posts I want you to employ and explore are all of equal value. One is not more valuable than the other. All of them together will guarantee your spiritual progress and success.

*Here are the **Five Cairns** that keep a spiritual life on track—if you pay attention. Paying attention is the simple definition of consciousness.*

LEARNING TO RECOGNIZE YOUR BELIEFS

Where did your beliefs about yourself and the world originate? Rules and traditions internalized become unconscious beliefs that push you around in your life with or without your permission.

We must ask ourselves; do these concepts still work for me?

Do they resonate as Truth for me?

Are they <u>shoulds</u>? (Shoulds are someone else's values.)

LEARNING TO TRUST YOUR INTUITION/YOUR KNOWING.

Your inner guidance... can you hear it?

Do you listen?

What price do you pay if you don't?

STILLNESS

Develop an ability to achieve 60 seconds of Stillness.

Are you allowing space/time for quiet in your day?

Can you still your mind for a minute?

If not, why?
And again, what price do you pay?

ACCEPTING LIFE IS TEMPORARY

*Living with uncertainty, we spend much
of our energy chasing security.
looking for guarantees.*

We try to numb the fear of "not knowing."

Learning to tolerate mystery is a big flipping deal.

How we accept life on life's terms is the key to peace.

ENLIVEN YOURSELF

Learning to give yourself experiences that enliven, invigorate and lift you. (Not alcohol or drug induced.)

*Experiencing joy, satisfaction, peace,
purpose, silliness, etc. are all signs
you are living authentically... consciously.*

So let me begin...
This is my story of living with and without consciousness...
with and without the use of cairns.

*"The events in our lives happen in time,
but in their significance to ourselves,
they find their own order...
the continuous thread of revelation."*
Eudora Welty

Chapter 1

My Tribe

I have been a therapist for over 30 years. I have been blessed to have worked with thousands of clients from all over the world. In many professions age is not seen as a benefit...that is not so for me as a therapist.

People want my experience and education. It has been an amazing career path. We teach what we need to learn and I have learned much from my clients, but no one taught me more than my mother.

I was named Irene for my maternal grandmother, who died when my mom was a child. Mom often forgot I was the daughter, not the mother. Mom was married six times, and we moved more times than that. She kept looking for the fairy tale life. When she had a husband, I was supposed to get in line, call the new man daddy, and join her fantasy family. Between husbands, she leaned on me as if I were an adult. Wherever we landed, we were immediately enrolled in the local public school and just as quickly, if not first, with the local Catholic parish. From her early childhood, Mom's refuge was the Roman Catholic Church, the church her father hated and forbid her to attend, the church my grandmother Irene loved. Irene was many years younger than my grandfather. They had an arranged marriage. I never met either my grandfather or obviously my grandmother. I only knew them from the stories my mother told and what I embellished. I have never met anyone from my biological father's family either; I heard even fewer stories about them. What I do have are my birth certificate and a baptism certificate. From these, I have the names of a few relatives.

Children take on the characteristics of the adults they know, their primary caregivers, and sub-consciously project them onto their idea of God. For me, God was, first of all, a man. He became a hybrid between the stories of my rage-filled grandfather and my life with step-fathers, sprinkled with some Santa Claus. In my head, this God sounded a lot like all the Catholic priests I had ever heard celebrate mass. God, the Father, was unpredictable and harsh. He offered NO slack. I mean... look at what he allowed for his son. As the story goes, he gave his only begotten son to the slaughter. What parent does that?! Like the principal in my elementary school, God was a presence I was aware of, but not someone I interacted with routinely. He was tucked away in an obscure office. Jesus was more like the assistant principal who was at recess and in the lunchroom.

The local parish priest, Father Whoever, was onboard to teach me God's rules. I was taught our priest, or *any* priest, knew what God wanted. Priests knew what God wanted not only for me but the world. They knew everything I needed to know to keep me in line on the straight and narrow. Father Whoever would let me know what was expected. I was convinced that if I followed the rules completely—to the letter—our lives would look a lot more like normal people. We would have enough money to pay bills, buy food and back-to-school clothes. Mom would no longer pick the wrong men to marry. She wouldn't be so unhappy. I reasoned that somehow other people knew how to keep God happy so bad things didn't happen to them. My mom and I were just not doing it the right way. Relentlessly, I worked on both of us, mom and me. And in turn, I worked on my younger sisters. Hence, I, the controlling co-dependent people pleaser, was created.

I needed the church to be right. I believed following the Right Way would make us all safe with the Almighty. The Right Way would protect us from our vulnerability and the whims of the heavy-handed God, Jesus' father. I needed the church to have answers. What were my questions?

Why didn't God give me a father who stayed? Why did Mom pick the wrong men to marry? Why didn't Jane's dad yell when Jane had all her noisy girlfriends over for a pajama party; while my step-father had his fists ready if we lifted our eyes at the dinner table? Why did Dale Kennedy think it was okay to try to convince Jane not to invite me to the big pajama party because I came from the wrong part of town?

God, where were you when the firemen came to the house on Christmas morning with a turkey and a box of cardboard checkers for me marked *"Girl age twelve"*? I hated the world that day. The firemen made it official. We were poor. Where was Santa Claus? What had I done wrong? What rule did I not follow? Why did Jane get her family and I got this one?

Sunday morning Mass provided answers. I got to feel special. I was being treated like Jesus. Through the stories of

Jesus and the saints, I learned how God made them suffer, especially his son. Jesus was God's favorite child, and for that honor, God let him hang on a cross and be tortured. WTF? I have never been quite sure why. Somehow Jesus would be sacrificed and give the rest of us a break? Really? Would we *all* be saved? I am still not sure how someone being martyred, (which I know is found throughout history in many religions) saves the rest of us. The message is a mystifying one for me.

But what I did interpret and hung onto for many years was the idea that God gave those he loved more burdens to carry than the normal folks. His *special ones* were given crosses to drag around. Big fat crosses were the sign of *"special."* This idea of special for many years kept me in situations trying to help, fix or change insanity that was not mine to do. It took me years to realize that I had to include considering myself in all my decisions. Once I learned to stay out of every drama I invited myself into, my life became so much healthier.

Every Sunday morning I listened to the stories of my mild mannered big brother Jesus, while I stared at him hanging on a cross with a crown of thorns and blood dripping from his body. I could relate to his life not being fair.

At mass when the priest moved to the lectern and opened the Bible to the Gospel lesson for the day, I paid attention. Different from the Protestant church where the minister's job performance is based on his sermons, the priest doesn't always have to preach a homily. As a kid, I remember many times that the priest only read from the script. No changes. But when he did preach, and when he explained the gospel, what I heard were stories about the

4

man Jesus. I loved the story of his virgin birth in a humble manger. I identified. We didn't own our home either. He was a teacher, and he loved children. There were no stories of his beating children or shaming them. He was a friend who didn't ignore people who were from the wrong side of town. He shared what he had and trusted there would be more. He went against authority. His parents gave him a lot of freedom. He believed in peace. Jesus was my hero. I loved him like the big brother I longed for as a kid. His importance was accentuated by the priest bowing down and kissing the Bible at the end of his reading and saying, "Thus saith the Lord."

But Jesus' heavenly Dad... now *he* was a different character and experience for me altogether. God, The Almighty Father... he scared me.

Question for you...

What scared you as a child?

Try not to ask yourself 'WHY was I scared' because WHY will always keep you in your head. Instead, ask yourself WHAT was I afraid of as a kid? Try to find a specific memory. And when you remember the what, where do you feel that in your body? Our bodies hold our memories.

Have you ever overreacted to a situation and while you are carrying on, some sane part of your brain will be letting you know that you are way overreacting? You hear the voice loud and clear and you know it is right but you don't stop.

The way I explain this to clients is first to reassure them that everyone does this at one time or another. We realize the situation, whatever it is, deserves maybe a cup full of feelings but we are giving it a truckload. What this reaction tells you is that you are standing right smack dab in the middle of your history.

Your reaction might be to freeze or withdraw, lose your voice, have your mind go blank. Or you scream and holler, become nasty and strike out like a cornered animal, possibly say things you later regret. Whatever way it manifests, I guarantee you are coming from an old place. A younger you is running the show.

The way to heal this is to see that younger you with compassion. Understand that you (as a child) were doing the best you knew how to at the time. Children are vulnerable and powerless.

Now breathe in deeply, close your eyes and see the younger you. The seeing may just be a feeling or it may be a vision of a time and place where you were frightened. Freeze the scene. Encourage the child to come with you to wherever you are safe today. Breathe. Just send compassion and love to yourself.

This is how to heal anything. You will know it has worked the next time you are in a situation that would have made you react like a crazy person and you don't. You give the experience only the cupful of emotion it deserves... it is healed.

I call this "catching yourself in a wave of health." It is a transformative, cool moment.

Space for notes to yourself...

Recognizing your beliefs
The first step to becoming conscious

It is essential to understand where your beliefs about yourself and the world originated.

Rules and traditions when internalized become solidified, turning into beliefs.

Beliefs push us around in our lives with or without our permission.

We need to ask ourselves do these concepts still work for me?

Do they resonate as Truth for me?

Are they shoulds? (Shoulds are someone else's values.)

*"Your beliefs pave your way to success
or block you."*
					Marsha Sinetar

Chapter 2

How Children Make God

God is a word we have all heard. Our conversations are laced with the word God; *"OMG"... "Thank God"... "For God's sake"... "In God we trust"... "God must have needed him more"... "God damn it"... "God forsaken place"*. Who or what are we talking about?

Your mom and dad were your first Gods. As a child, you created *psychological stickers* from the behaviors of your parents or guardians. You used those stickers to create your picture of God. You embellished your picture with some bits of Santa Claus and monsters from under the bed. You then hung your picture on the door of your heart. Over the years, as you grew, you added to the picture.

Even if your parents were atheists and convinced you there was no God, you still made your picture. You used what you heard to create your image. Did you hear statements like?

"We don't believe in a man in the sky who controls everything."

"We don't believe there's a devil that will make you burn in hell."

"We don't believe in an afterlife, this life is it."

All of it, everything you heard or imagined, you used to create the God of your understanding. It all morphed into your beliefs about God. It all became your God picture. Unless you have opened it to the light, that image with the corners curled from age is still hanging on your heart,.

> ***Rules and traditions become beliefs.***
> ***Beliefs are what motivate our life choices.***

Here is an example: A 38 year old client remembers that as a child she had to be a good girl in order to please her parents. If she didn't, her punishments were harsh. Her mom went from ignoring her to beating her. She seldom felt safe. This little girl convinced herself that in order to be safe she had to remain vigilant. She must be perfect. She grew to expect perfection from herself. If her parents were angry and she suffered consequences, she blamed them on herself. This is what children do. When life is dysfunctional at home or out of control, children make themselves wrong. Subconsciously it gives them an illusion of control. I can't make my caregivers change. I have to change me.

Today this wonderful woman recognizes that she translated her belief of "not being good enough" to holding herself up to a standard of needing to be 100% right, perfect all the time. She allowed herself no slack. There can't be dishes in the sink. No room for errors at work–no matter how slight. Everyone she was involved with must be happy. The standard she operated under was 100% perfect or nothing. The nothing resulted in collapse...hanging out on the couch, eating junk food, bingeing on TV. She would give up under a cloud of self-criticism and shame.

As an adult and out from under the pressure of her parents she was able to own her childhood story. She worked in therapy to feel the feelings, find compassion for herself and move on to defining and creating her experience and connection to the Divine. My client has been able to find the God of her understanding. The connection she has today with her spirituality is rich and full. Spiritual growth is constantly evolving...moving. It is the blood of our life energy.

Does she ever fall back into old behaviors? Yes of course...we all do.

The big difference is now she recognizes what she is doing and with her awareness she is able to turn things around much quicker. Her behavior is no longer a mystery to her. She has the power to change.

Questions for you...

What God did you create as a child?

What beliefs about God did you bring away from childhood?

The enemy is fear. We think it is hate; but, it is fear.
Gandhi

Chapter 3

My Safe Place

During my high school years, sophomore, junior and senior, I helped my mother bury two husbands. Jack died after being my stepfather for eight years and the father of my little sister Jackie. The next husband, Stewart, and mom were married for six months when he dropped dead on our sun porch in my sister Dorothy's arms. I was embarrassed that our neighbors once again felt compelled to make more casseroles for us.

I took my feelings and questions to morning Mass. Saint Martha's Roman Catholic Church was three miles from our house. Often, I walked there when I didn't have a ride. Morning Mass was my safe place. It was quiet, always predictable. No one ever moved the furniture or changed the script. On Easter, the altar was decorated with white lilies. On Christmas, the altar guild ladies brought in red poinsettias. Like clockwork, there were designated vestments for ordinary days, high holy days, funerals and weddings, no mixing or matching. Each celebration had its own outfit. The altar boys wore black floor-length garments with white overlays. The Latin mumbling and chanting found its daily rhythm—nothing changed for 2000 years, or so they said. I breathed in the familiarity. The tradition, structure, and quiet held me like a pool float in the middle of the deep waters of life.

Nothing changed until 1962 when the Vatican II Council finished their assembly. The furniture was moved. They turned the priest and the altar around. The priest was now facing the congregation during the entire Mass. And he started reading that same Mass in English. I loved it. Life was changing. It was the sixties. These changes made the church more user-friendly. I liked my church even better. However, there was one little crack in the perfect chalice. That fissure was the whole fish on Friday issue. They changed the rules! How come if it was a venial sin last week to eat meat on Friday—this week you can have a hamburger? It's not a problem? What? Really? It's okay now? Ugh, does that make this rule arbitrary? Arbitrary is not perfect, not black and white.

Did God have a bone to pick with the fishermen? (I couldn't stop myself from the pun.) What did God's memo say? How did he justify the rule change? Thinking about it made me uncomfortable. The idea of this break in tradition irritated the back of my brain like a tag on the neck of a new shirt.

As I write this I am thinking of the way things are now in 2016. The Supreme Court has ruled marriage is legal for same-sex couples, transgender people have rights, and women can fight on the front lines of combat, to name just a few.

Now the rules are changing at lightning speed. There

has always been change, but not at the rapid pace of today. Some are protesting the changes while others are celebrating. The many who are delighted, see them as progress. While just as many are sure the world-order is coming to an end; at least the world as they know it. Most of the cultural rule changes happening today are not scaring me, but I can understand the fear that others have. I remember the time in my life when I wanted the rules. They gave me an illusion of safety.

Rules are black and white. Rules numb the fear of uncertainty. They distract us from the reality that nothing is permanent on planet earth. Human beings crave the familiar more than anything. Often we go to what we know rather than a change that would bring us happiness. I see this so often in clients who want to try a new job, or want to leave or enter a different relationship, want to try a new place or way of living. They may want to challenge parents with their wedding plans or how they raise the grandchildren. You know what I am talking about. We all have struggled with the discomfort of change. And we have all, at one time or another, lived with the pain of staying in the status quo because of fear of change. Change brings an unknown.

Change calls up all our defenses. Rules are the language of status quo. They give us a rope of control that is tied in nothing more solid than air. Life is motion...movement. Life is a current constantly flowing. We often stay in boats tied up to familiar docks because we are afraid of the waves that casting off in a new direction will cause. ***Learning to tolerate and find peace with the unknown is a big challenge for us earthlings.***

(This is a cairn)

So now you have the back story. Picture it... June of 1963. I was 17 and about to hold a diploma in my hand. I had enrolled into our Lady of Fatima Hospital School of Practical Nursing. I would be studying with the nuns. I wanted a good-paying trade. I wanted to be self-supporting and on my own as quickly as possible. Once I completed the program, I was going to buy a VW bug and drive across the country. I'd get a job in a hospital in California, somewhere far away. The L.P.N. program was eighteen months long and cheap. I had received 99% on the entrance exam. I knew I could do it. I wanted out from under the responsibility of being my mother's daughter. I had saved the money and freedom was soon to be parked in the driveway.

Let me introduce Mr. Robbins, my Civics teacher. He believed in me. Without any information about my home life, Mr. R. meant well. He saw my plan as selling myself short. He wanted a bigger goal for me. Mom was summoned to his office. There we sat and listened while Mr. R. argued for me to withdraw from Our Lady of Fatima. With his connections he could get me into Cape Cod Community College. This discussion was happening two weeks before my graduation. He sold me his plan. He assured me I could swing the tuition. After two years he saw no reason why I wouldn't get a scholarship to B.U. or one of the many four-year colleges in Boston. Mom, of course agreed. Yes, that was it. You need to understand that if Mr. R. had told my mother I needed to walk on crushed glass for the next two years, she would have run to get a hammer and some empty milk bottles. Teachers and priests were my mother's gods. They were her Higher Power and consequently, mine.

Flattered by Mr. R's attention I shut off the voice/

intuition/knowing that was reminding me, "No, this isn't your plan." I dismissed MY dream. I chastised myself for having such a small goal. What was I trying to do... take the easy way out? Declaring me lazy, off I went to write the withdrawal letter.

> **Some of my beliefs—the rules:**
> **Teachers, priests...someone else knew best**
> **and**
> **Difficult was always the better choice.**
> **God didn't like easy.**

At 17 my head and heart were filled with rules. Freshly graduated from high school, I saw possibility for my life, everywhere. I fervently believed if I followed the rules, thus making me a *good girl;* God would be pleased, and my life was guaranteed to work out.

During the summer of 1963, I met Kevin, a handsome cop who was nine years older than me. I was 17 and he was 26. I worked the 10 p.m. to 6 a.m. shifts at the Route One Diner and Lounge. Kevin came in regularly with his partner for coffee and a cigarette. We started dating.

What happened once I started school and was living on Cape Cod? Well, the short version is Kevin hounded me to quit school and marry him. He saw no need for me to have a college education. Why did I need a degree? He was doing just fine with only a high school diploma.

Then there was my mother. Daily she called me crying about how much she missed me. She threatened, if I was going to keep going out with this boyfriend of mine she wasn't wasting any of her money on me. At the time she was sending me $10 a week to supplement my board. I was cleaning for a local woman but I wasn't making enough to cover all my expenses.

Two strong feelings had my attention. The first feeling was *JOY*. I loved college, all of it. I liked my friends, being elected to the student government council and being away from my mother. My second feeling was *GUILT*. Honor thy father and mother–what about my poor mom? And Kevin... what about Kevin? He and I were getting really close to *going all the way*.

Given time I might have worked through the honor thy mother and father thing. But sex... intercourse outside of marriage... NO WAY...TOO BIG. We are talking a lightning strike to the back of my curly (then) strawberry blonde head. I didn't trust myself to stay a virgin. My housemates were going all the way. What did they know? They were Protestants. I couldn't. I just couldn't. I knew the rules. No sex before marriage and no birth control. Sex was for making babies. Father Salmon said so.

Questions for you...

Where in your life do you cling to rules or try to find stability in tradition/sameness?

What is your relationship to resistance right now in your life?

What rules were governing your sexual behavior as a kid?

Whose rules were they... yours... your parents... your church... the other kids?

As a kid did you know about your intuition?

Oh, the places you will go if you don't learn to
Trust What You Know.

Chapter 4

What Will People Think?

Rules challenge intuition.
Intuition challenges the rules.

The date was Friday, February 14, 1964. It was 5 p.m. and I was at St. Martha's Roman Catholic Church in Plainville, Massachusetts. It was a cold, dark evening. The sky was beginning to fill with thick snowflakes. The church parking lot was collecting the flakes quickly. The arriving cars marked the accumulating depth.

"Do you guys have a scraper?" Kevin asked. "By the time I get out of here I'm gonna' need one."

Kevin didn't have an ice scraper and he didn't have a topcoat, and of course, no gloves. He did, however, have his brown and white pack of Camels and his silver flip top lighter. Everything about Kevin was thick, not fat–thick. Twenty-seven years old, thick auburn red hair, thick hands with thick nicotine stained fingers. His thick neck supported his thick square face. His thick shoulders supported his best navy blue suit. His skinny blue tie pointed to his closed button down collared shirt; there was no missing his thick chin waiting to be released.

God, I remember him clearly, but where am I? What am I wearing? I can see my feet. I was always wearing spike heels, trying to look older. I know they had to be black– not a doubt. I can remember slipping on the slush-covered asphalt.

Kevin held my arm with his right hand. With his left hand he protected his ever-present lit Camel cigarette. Keeping his cigarette dry from the falling snow, we carefully walked across the parking lot maneuvering our best dress up shoes through the piling slush.

I still can't see what I had on. What was I wearing? I know what I wore the next day. But what did I wear that Friday night—the rehearsal night.

I had to be wearing the new black wool coat with a mink Peter Pan collar. I bought it for the occasion. I also know that my head was covered with my Jackie-Kennedy-at-the-funeral black lace mantilla look-alike. That was the official head gear for the cool Catholic girls in 1964. But what was I wearing? I can't remember my dress. I can remember how I felt. I didn't want to be there. I wanted everyone to go home. I wanted to be brave enough to call the whole thing off. I wanted not to feel responsible for the 125 stuffed chicken breasts that were reserved for the next day. I wanted Father Salmon to know the truth.

At 18 I just wanted to find out what sex was about. I didn't want to rehearse anything. I didn't want to hear the Ave Maria. I didn't want to get married. I wanted to go back to college. I wanted to drive a VW across the United States. I wanted to work in California and then maybe join the Air Force and let them pay for me to train as a registered nurse.

I was rehearsing the wedding my mother never had. The wedding wasn't what I wanted. I wanted an education. I wanted to see California. I wanted to travel. I wanted to be back at Cape Cod Community College or Lady of Fatima Nursing School. I wanted to transfer to B.U. I wanted my mother to let me be at college without calling me daily to tell me how lonely she was and how she needed me to come home. I wanted her to stop crying. I wanted her to get a life and stop using mine. I wanted my little sisters not to be afraid because I wasn't home. I wanted Kevin to stop being jealous of the guys at school. I wanted him to stop hounding me. I wanted Father Salmon to understand my growing sexuality. I wanted the Catholic Church to cut me some slack. I wanted to be a kid. And I didn't want to let God down.

On Saturday, February 15, 1964 at 10 a.m. at Saint Martha's church in Plainville, Massachusetts, I smiled for the wedding photographer. I kept it up all day long.

Learn to trust your Intuition/your Knowing
Your inner guidance... can you hear it?
Do you listen?

All of the spiritual masters/teachers encourage us to 'be still and know.' I don't think the knowing is always the difficult step. I believe the trusting what we know and then acting on it is the challenge. Every cell in my body screamed at me to NOT get married. I remember so clearly that my KNOWING was convinced marrying Kevin was a big mistake. My FEAR would have none of it. Fear was spraying me with "SHOULDS." I should keep my word. Look at all the people I would let down. I should be married if I want to be sexual. People have spent money and time on me. I owe. I should be considerate. What would people think? What would we do with the 125 baked stuffed chicken breasts that had been ordered? Suck it up, girl. As mom would say, "You made your bed, now lie in it."

Questions for you...

Think of a time you did not listen to your Intuition... your Knowing.

What were the consequences?

The truth will set you free but first it will piss you off.
-Phyllis Diller-

Chapter 5

Split

It was 1967. My daughters were 2 and 3 when the front page of the local newspaper pictured a young mom being arrested for the murder of her husband. The story alleged that she had picked up a knife from her dish rack before the husband could get one more punch to her face. With her back pressed hard against her kitchen counter she stuck the knife in his belly. He was dead when the police arrived.

A second photograph showed her two young children being shuffled into a vehicle that was clearly designated official with the seal of the Commonwealth of Massachusetts. That photograph sent a chill of warning though my blood. I knew how the woman in the newspaper felt. I prayed for her safety. I heeded the warning.

I knew what motivated that woman. I knew how she summoned up enough hate to stick a knife in her drunken husband. When a man insane with alcohol and stronger than you is punching your face and head, every instinct in your body wants to find a way to hurt him back. The warrior in the bottom of my belly identified with the front page mother.

My husband Kevin was a local cop. Cops protect their own. If he was in our town he never received citations for his drunk driving. The few times I called them to the house they told me to leave until he sobered up. They chastised me for making such a big deal of our "domestic problems." Those two newspaper pictures terrified me. I could be in the paper next. I didn't want my children in a sheriff's car. I never wanted my children taken away from me. I feared that if I fought back I would find myself in handcuffs in the backseat of a police cruiser.

Barely three weeks late again Kevin was sleeping off a drunken stupor. The house was quiet with the deafening silence that follows a night of domestic violence. My face throbbed. My right eye was swollen almost shut. My balance was thrown off by my impaired vision. What was I going to do? I didn't want this life for my girls. I needed help. I wanted someone to tell me how to make Kevin stop drinking and how to stop the craziness at our house. I had to make my marriage work. I was willing to do whatever it took. I called the only resource I knew to call; the place I had gone for answers and rules my whole life.

The following happened before I had any consciousness of the cairns I now live my life by.

"Hi, my name is Irene, and I take Communion at your church. I was wondering if I could have an appointment today with one of the priests."

"Could you please tell me what this is in regards to?"

"It's about my marriage. My husband and I are having some problems. I really need to talk to a priest today."

"Okay, well, what about one o'clock. He'll see you at the rectory right after his lunch. Can you make it then?"

I said I'd be there, thanked the female voice and hung up. I put the girls in the stroller and walked the two miles to the local rectory. I needed to talk to the priest.

My face hurts. The conversation in my head pulsated. *God, I hate walking up to the church looking like this, even with sunglasses and a hat. Irene, get over it. Very few people in this town know you. You haven't been here a year yet. They won't notice. Oh, my eye is so sore. I'll put more ice on it later.*

"Mommy boo-boo? Daddy hit? No, no hit."

"Daddy is sorry honey. Daddy no hit anymore."

I hate Kevin right now. Oh God, I never wanted my girls to see this. I never wanted them to have this craziness in their home. Nice job, Irene. You've given the girls what you grew up in. They don't deserve to live like this. They don't deserve drunken rages waking everyone up in the night, hearing their mom being pushed around—the hitting and kicking. The priest will help. He will guide me. He will give me direction. I just need to hang on until I see him.

"Hello, Father, I'm Irene. These are my two girls. Lynn is three years old and Shawn Mary is two."

"Well, hello girls. You certainly have your hands full. Now, have you been in my office before? Do we know each other?"

"Not really Father, but I have been receiving Holy Communion here for about a year. I came from St Martha's church with Father Salmon."

"Oh, yes, Father Salmon. He's in a retirement home now. Did you know that?"

"Yes Father, my mother told me."

"So, what is it I can do for you? What happened to your face?"

"Well, Father, that's why I'm here. My husband's done this to me a couple of times. He comes home drunk and goes into a rage. I've come to ask your guidance."

"Well, my dear, what have you done to make him so angry?"

WHAT?! WHAT HAVE I DONE TO MAKE HIM ANGRY!!!

My mind snapped. I went black with rage and my voice froze. I fell into a black hole... a void.

He did not just say that. He couldn't have just said that. I am here because all of my life, I have done everything his church has told me to do. And this is what he says to me? What have I done to make my husband so angry? Not as much as I would like to do to you, you bastard!

I have no idea what else he said. I think he mumbled something about praying to the Blessed Mother. Maybe I just made that up. I wanted out. I wanted out of his office. I wanted out of that building. I wanted out of that church. I wanted out of my marriage. And I wanted out of any further relationship with God.

That day I drew a line in the sand, a line that would mark the very place I would build a solid wall. Kevin, my marriage, the Catholic Church, and God were on one side of the line. The girls and I were on the other.

I felt like one of those old ladies in Florida. You know the ones you read about who turn their whole life savings, every penny over to a con-man. This bastard convinced our old friend that she could double her money ...or she could use her money to help Jesus... or feed starving children. Who knows what the cons might have promised? I have no facts. But I bet you my last bite of Ben and Jerry's the old lady's gut, belly, red flag detector was blaring and she didn't want to hurt someone's feelings. So she dismissed what her gut was screaming at her. She did not want to believe that these cons were going to hurt her. She didn't want to hurt their feelings. She didn't know how to speak up or find her voice. She didn't want to make a scene. She just ignored her intuition... her KNOWING. Instead she went and got her checkbook. I on the other hand was afraid to bolt the night of my wedding rehearsal when every fiber of my being screamed I was making a mistake. After all what would my mom do with the 125 stuffed chicken breasts that were waiting for the oven at Sandy's Restaurant the next day?

My experience of feeling wronged by the church and its teachings would be labeled by psychologists as a "*break in belonging.*" A break in belonging is the moment when our foundation of safety and trust–***our core beliefs***–are flipped upside down. The moment we get slapped with a reality we didn't see coming. Leaving us stripped naked in the void. We are no longer able to cover ourselves with the soothing comfort of our black and white beliefs.

Questions for you...

Are you reminded of an experience of not listening to your intuition, your gut?

What stopped you?

How did this decision not to heed your inner guidance affect your life?

How did the memory make you feel?

Holding onto anger is like taking poison
and expecting the other person to die.
                              -Buddha-

Chapter 6

Getting Myself Ex-communicated

I was mad. No, I was madder than mad. I was enraged. I wanted to punch, scream, and stomp. I wanted to strike back. There was nothing to hit. The frustration pulsed in my molecules. I rattled with tension. How do you kick God in the groin? How do you give God the finger? How do you get back opportunity? I wanted to put two little girls back into my womb and tell them to wait there while I get us a life. I have to run back and get an education and pick up the youth I left behind. I'll be back. You wait right here, and when I'm grown up enough to be a Mom and breadwinner, I'll be back to get you. I was staring at the smashed one-of-a-kind antique crystal goblet called my youth. I had dropped it on the floor. It was shattered... irreplaceable. It was gone. My young adult years were broken into a million pieces. I had to sweep up the shards and move on.

I walked home from the church in a stunned shock. Floating on a sea of betrayal, trapped in a void with no exits, my rage began turning inward. How could I have been so stupid? None of my college friends had bought this virginity mandate... sex only for making babies bull shit. How could I have screwed myself so badly and worse yet, how could I have brought two precious little girls into this mess? I was devastated. For the first time in my life, I had nowhere to go. I had always had the church. I had always had God.

God was dead to me. He and his men in black could all go f@#& themselves. I was never doing business with the old men's club again. My hands, which had so often been in prayer position, were now clenched into fists. Inflamed, I called the priest at the local Episcopal church.

I know, at first you may see this action as a complete about face. Hold on, let me explain. This was how I could slap God and "HIS" church in the face. Remember, as a Catholic we were not allowed to even enter another church without incurring sin on our souls. I wasn't just entering. I had phoned the enemy Church to begin the process of being converted to the Episcopal faith. I didn't want to be a lapsed Catholic. I wanted ex-communication. I wanted an official divorce from the *Church*. This was the only way I knew how to do it. I would do the unspeakable; I would become one of them. Kevin had been raised Episcopalian, so I had a tiny bit of familiarity with this church. Pretty much all I knew was where the building was and the name of the minister. Episcopal ministers are also called priests like their Catholic counterparts. They also wear the black shirts with white collars. The similarities end there.

The classes were free, and the priest became my first counselor. He was a married man which made him human to me, much different than the clergy I had known throughout my childhood. He explained the wall of bitterness I was forming around my heart was not going to serve my children or me. He helped me to believe there was light at the end of the dark night that I was living. He was the first sighting of land I could see from the shipwreck I was floating on.

Through the classes, I began to learn the history of Christianity and why the Anglican Church split from Rome. I learned about the Reformation, Martin Luther, and what some of the major philosophical differences were separating the Catholics from the Protestants. Thus, began my lifelong fascination with religious history, world religions, and ultimately philosophy.

While enrolled in the conversion class I made one last trip to a local Catholic Church. Like a jilted lover I had to ride by his house one more time to see if his car was there. I don't know what I expected to feel, experience or find. I entered the cool sanctuary on a Saturday afternoon. I knew the doors would be unlocked and parishioners would be taking confession. I slid into an empty pew in the back of the church. Automatically I genuflected and reached down to drop the kneeler to the floor as I slumped to my knees, all programmed habits as familiar as brushing my teeth. I looked at the altar. It looked the same as every other Catholic church I had ever been in, but *I* wasn't the same. I was like a wounded soldier returning from war realizing that his sacrifice was in vain. It didn't matter. The soldier recognized his sacrifice changed nothing in the world. They were still fighting, people were still being slaughtered, and he was alive with nothing but a lost limb to show for his efforts. I was identifying with the Vietnam soldiers who were coming back home to America. (Today it would be the Iraq/Afghanistan troops.) Like them, I thought I had to be one of the good guys. I had done what they told me was the right thing. I had followed the instructions of my elders, the people in the know.

I longed for an answer, a voice of apology, or recognition–something. There was silence, nothing but the glow of the votive remembrance candles and the shuffle of feet as parishioners moved in and out of the confessional booths. It was over. All the safety I had perceived, the hours of guidance I had clung to, the trust I had spent were all over–finished. I cried from the deepest place I had ever touched inside myself. I cried until I was blinded by the heat of my tears. I sobbed until I was empty, until the ooze of black hate started to trickle into the newly emptied space. The hate filled me like air fills a steel spiked snow tire. The hate lifted me to sit straight up. I was lifted off my knees. My hate was completely offended that I was on my knees. My back arched. I was on my feet. Standing in the middle of the aisle facing the altar, I deliberately exited without making the sign of the cross.

Anger is a feeling, but it is always connected to sadness, hurt, and/or fear.

Until we learn to feel it all, we don't finish it. Feelings are meant to be finished. They let us know how an experience has landed on us. We need to feel, express and move on. I would not allow myself to feel the fear, sadness, and hurt under my anger. The results of unfinished anger are resentment and bitterness. I was stuck in the resentment for a very long time.

For those of you who won't do the anger but rather stay in the fear, sadness and/or hurt–your consequence is depression.

Questions for you...

Where are you stuck?
Literally, not just what are you stuck about, but where in your body do you feel it? Say "why," then breathe slowly into your body.

Where does your breath hesitate? This hesitation will give you a clue to where your feelings are hung up. When we allow ourselves to hang out in these uncomfortable places we can begin to finish our feelings. Just notice.

Some of us can do the anger, but not the hurt or fear. We have no tolerance for the vulnerability.

Some of us hang on to the hurt or fear but won't touch the anger. We may have seen anger or more likely violence as a child and swore we would never go there. Either way, we don't finish the feelings and we stay jammed, not able to access all that we are.

We can let our lives be directed by the same forces that make flowers grow or we can do it ourselves.
-Marianne Williamson-

Chapter 7

Moving On... But Where Am I Going?

I did leave Kevin. Under the advisement of my attorney, I didn't tell Kevin I was going. My attorney told me to take whatever I could while Kevin was at work because I would have no rights to anything if we went to court. It was 1967. I was not quite 21 years old. His name was on everything legal. Married women were not allowed to have even as much as the phone bills in their names...no credit of their own...NOTHING. I, of course, never questioned any of this for many reasons. First, it was the culture at the time, and that culture was reinforced by my religion which did not recognize women as equal to men. Women had to cover their heads in the house of God. Women had no seat at the table in any of the church hierarchy. They were forbidden in any part of the decision making. Women were second class citizens. They had no more authority than children. As the thinking went, if God wanted women involved then Jesus would have had female disciples. (Note: Men were the only ones allowed to vote on what stories would or would not be in the Bible. I would call that a biased editorial board. Some historians say there are stories that demonstrated that Jesus did use women for counsel.)

Mom's last husband, John, was well aware of the domestic violence in my marriage. More than once he unsuccessfully tried to encourage Kevin to stop his drinking and violent outbursts. We all knew that only Kevin could change his drinking. On the night I moved, John and Mom came with a truck. They waited out of sight until they saw Kevin leave for work. He worked the second shift at the General Motors plant as a security guard. He carried a gun. When we were confident that Kevin was gone, we began throwing everything as fast as we could into the truck.

Terror and rage filled my bloodstream. I was as disconnected during the move as I was after the priest asked me to explain what made my husband so angry. I was numb like a soldier in the battlefield; just managing one foot in front of the other. The main goal was to survive. Kevin would be furious when he got home to an empty house. I left him his easy chair, our bed, and dresser (which later I realized had all the girls' baby pictures in the top drawer). I left him some dishes and enough kitchen supplies to function.

I not only felt terror and rage, I also felt sorry for Kevin. I knew he would be hurt and lost. He had been a product of the Massachusetts foster care system. Abandonment was an old wound for him. If I had not had children, I most likely would have stayed in that marriage longer. At the time I had no idea that I deserved better, but I had no doubt that my girls did. I could not let them have one more violent night of mommy getting punched and daddy throwing beer bottles. We were done. I left without a dime. I didn't even have pocket change. We went to my mom's new address with my step-father and their combined brood of five kids living at home. It was insane. The girls and I lasted there for six crazy months until I found a job and a place for us to stay. At my first job I earned $87 a week. Childcare was $40 weekly. The ratio is not much different today for many single moms or dads.

After some difficult false starts, I was able to secure an apartment in Roxbury, Massachusetts. In 1968 and 1969, Roxbury was a predominately black community. It was the only place I could afford the rent, and landlords allowed children. In those days landlords could discriminate against children as they can now against dogs. I was grateful to have it. I found a United Way day care center for my girls. The center offered a sliding fee scale. Soon, I was hired there as a teacher's helper. Through the daycare center I was connected to a grant offered by President Lyndon Johnson's Great Society Program. I began taking college courses in education.

I started to build my life on rage and determination. There were more feelings, but those were the only two I allowed myself to acknowledge. Unconsciously, I cut myself off from my fear. I didn't understand what I was doing. I had myself convinced I had no fear. I was not able to let the fear surface. I had to keep putting one foot in front of the other. My fear was buried. I defaulted to numb. Numb for me was an old childhood coping mechanism. It was like using my right hand. I had done it for so long I had no idea the fear was there. I judged others who showed their fear and vulnerability. I saw them as weak and with bad attitudes. "Get over your–self," I growled inside my thoughts. Buck up. If I couldn't let me have my fear, I sure couldn't let you have yours. How did I stay numb? I did it by picking up alcohol...cheap fruity wine–sangria to be exact. I wanted to get my daily serving of vitamin C. Yeah...right...like I was worried about nutrition. I didn't want to feel.

I was 21 and missing all the parties that my friends were having at college. I *deserved* my comfort. Evenings I would pour myself the famous "a glass of wine" while I fed, bathed, read to my girls and put them to bed. I became obsessed with getting a college degree. At night, I filled my glass and read. I would give myself just another *splash* of wine and get the laundry going. I just *splashed* my way to slurring my words and stumbling to bed. I wasn't hurting anyone, so I told myself. I was taking myself off duty... I was relaxing.

My career path was decided by a government grant. I would get a degree in Education, Early Childhood Education to be exact. Now I had two new Gods to lean on–alcohol and education. At the time I had no idea that I had replaced my Catholic God with alcohol and education. And if you had brought it to my attention I would have suggested that you had your head up an anatomically impossible orifice. For the first time in my life I was taking charge, and no one was going to tell me anything different. My rage gave me an illusion of empowerment. I fueled my determination with it. Alcohol and then cigarettes gave me the illusion of courage. I kept myself completely disconnected from any feelings. It's just so ironic that here I would sit 48 years later, a therapist and life coach teaching clients about feelings. (Goes to show you we teach what we most need to learn.)

Kevin visited the girls a few times, making plans with them and failing to follow through. Soon he stopped making plans. There was one child support payment and then no more. My fate became clear. I would do this on my own, thank you very much. Along with my determination... my bitterness grew.

For the next 17 years I used Kevin as my definition of an alcoholic. I compared my drinking to his. He lost jobs, totaled cars, got arrested for D.W.I. I never lost a job because of my drinking. I paid my bills and took care of my girls. I didn't get bagged for a D.W.I. (Not for lack of trying. I drove many times during those 17 years under the influence. There were times in my arrogance I made myself the designated driver. I definitely had angels watching over me.)

Driving while intoxicated was not the only way I put myself in danger. Oh no. I was hell bent on making up for my lost "youth." It was the sixties. All the rules were being ripped up and stomped on, as an army of women marched over the pieces on their way to equality. Dressed in my self-righteous bitterness, accessorized with white-imitation-leather go-go boots and an I.U.D, I joined the parade. I was off and running to the sexual revolution. Done with the sex-only-when-married pledge of my youth, I was thumbing my nose at the Catholic Church. I did everything but call the Pope and asked him to come and watch me now.

So what did a day (or should I say night) in my life as a sixties' female sexual revolutionist look like? Let's see... I would start the day around 5 a.m. with a large glass of orange juice and one lovely little supplement known on the streets as Mother's Little Helper or Black Beauties. In the pharmaceutical world, my new little Gods were known as amphetamines–the pure, golden profit maker. These sweet little babies gave me all the energy I would need for the next

24 hours with the bonus of taking away my appetite. Ahh... it was perfect. I had no need for food, and I could always count on fitting into my skinny bell-bottom pants. I was cooking. With my little pharmaceutical helpers, I was able to get it all done.

I could be a single mom, work at the day-care center 40 hours a week, attend college classes two nights a week, get my papers written and keep a 4.0 G.P.A. After the girls were tucked into bed for the night with the babysitter plunked in front of our black and white TV, I was ready to go out bar hopping with my friends. As they say in A.A., *I was dressed up to get messed up.* I joined the other feminine revolutionists in the great American pastime–"hooking up". The bars would close around 1 a.m., and then I would schlep my perky, bug-eyed self home to have more wine. I needed to shut my racing brain-engine off. My goal was to get 2 or 3 hours of sleep so that I might begin the insanity again at 5 a.m.

Questions for you...

Can you relate?

Relate because you behaved this way?
Or feel like you missed something because you didn't behave the same way?

Relate sometimes means you understand or recognize the feelings, not necessarily the same circumstances.
Just notice.

Life is a succession of lessons
which must be lived to be understood.
-Helen Keller-

Chapter 8

A Functioning Alcoholic Is Born

Producing, playing, planning, pushing–constantly moving. This pace was my life. I filled every moment with activity. I was running as fast as I could. But I didn't know where I was going, or more worrisome I didn't know where I could stop. Where was the finish line? There was no finish line–no end. I kept moving it to the next course.. next program... next book to read... bill I needed to pay... clothes the girls needed... holiday to get through... presents to wrap... muffler to be replaced... parent/teacher meeting. I was grabbing for time. Life was one giant to-do list. Big goals... little goals... get them done... find the money... find the time... figure it out... keep moving.. .another glass of wine... you deserve it.... keep moving... where did I put my matches?

I got a lot done. I juggled many balls successfully. Yet there were two areas of my life–rest and introspection–that received none of my attention. Hell, I had no clue what introspection was, and I had no patience with even the idea of rest. Rest seemed to be a big waste of time. Come on.

I prided myself on overcoming the need for rest. Look

how much I was getting done. I was making something of myself. I was making up for lost time. I wouldn't stop. But now, from my "old lady" vantage point, looking through the rearview mirror of my life, I can see that if I stopped–sat with stillness–I would have had to feel. Stillness would require feeling. Feeling could wreak all kinds of havoc. A "Self" inside of me might begin to ask questions. Questions I had never taken seriously. Questions like, "What do I want? What calls to me? How do I fit into the big picture? What IS the big picture?" I was a fast moving to-do list maker. I just grabbed the 'whatever' in front of me and made the best of them. I applauded myself for being resourceful. I was making things work… making lemonade (or vodka and lemonade) out of lemons.

I was not creating a life from my intuition, from my deep Knowing. I didn't have time to go deep. I was running away from what I didn't want. I didn't want to need any help. I wanted to do it on my own. I wasn't going to trust or need anyone again. I acted needless and wantless. I rejected anything that touched my vulnerability.

Living from what we don't want is a reaction. It keeps us stuck in our past. We continue to point our finger back at what we hated about our past. Declaring, "I will have no more of that!" We react by doing the opposite. I had no education. So, I'll get an education, damn it. I had grim determination. The idea of wanting an education in and of itself was okay, but it wasn't complete. What education do I want? How do I want to use my gifts and talents? What are they? What am I being called to do? Those are deep questions that lie beneath our consciousness. What is my "Self?" Self with a capital S. Self with a capital S is an inside resident. A person has to slow down and look inside. No way did I ever take a moment to practice introspection.

My "Mother's Little Helpers," and my dear friends the "Black Beauties" gave me the first clue my life was out of control. Throughout the day my tongue kept sticking to the roof of my mouth. Not only did my little pharmaceutical helpers take my appetite away, but they made it almost impossible for me to drink water. I would gag. Just putting anything in my mouth during the day would force a gag response. I know, what's to complain about? This was such a small price to pay to live in skinny jeans. Or so I thought, until one moment—a frozen moment in time.

The moment... a core life scene that hasn't faded, never went away. It is a picture hanging in the hallway of my consciousness. The girls were about 4 and 5. They were in bed, and I was in for the night. It must have been a Monday night which was my sacred night, my high holy night, the night I took my weekly break from scooping. Scooping in 1969 in Boston among my friends meant finding guys. Now I think it's called Tinder. So, a scoop-free evening included doing my laundry, shaving my legs, plucking my eyebrows... you get it. I took my glass of wine into the bathroom (more like a closet with a tub and toilet). I turned on the water and watched it rush to fill the tub. I put the seat down on the toilet. I sat there for a moment while watching the water swirl. I picked up a plastic bottle of Minnie Mouse Bubble Bath and dumped 1/4 of its contents into the whirlpool. The bubbles quickly began to form and rise. They called me into the bath. I pulled off my clothes and stepped into the hot steamy water. The bubbles were in charge. I was at their mercy.

The bathroom was not a place I hung out. In and out, just get it done. But on this particular Monday night, I sat soaking. The glass of wine was comfortably within reach on the toilet seat. All my focus rested on the rising bubbles. I sat there long enough for the water to cool. My bare shoulders began to chill. I wanted to cry. My eyes longed to cry. My shoulders were heavy with tears. My heart ached... and NOTHING. My being had turned into Styrofoam. It was dry, stiff, brittle, and jammed. Nothing would express. Just stuck. I sat stuck, stuck, stuck. And there in the stillness, I received a gift of light. I saw the dead end street down which the Black Beauties had led. I felt fear. Something inside my chest (not my head) snapped. In a flash, I got up, dripping and cold. I quickly opened the medicine cabinet door, grabbed the amber plastic bottle, lifted the toilet lid and flushed my "Mothers' Little Helpers" down... down into the Roxbury, Massachusetts municipal sewer system. I knew that if I didn't act immediately, I wouldn't do it. Something inside me... *something that loved me had my attention*. For one blazing moment of light, I listened to my inner guidance.

I had no idea how the impetus got into my bathwater, or for that matter, into me. Maybe it was brought to me through the wonderful world of Disney via my Minnie Mouse Bubble Bath. It sure as hell did not come through my glass of wine. If anything, my old pal wine ordinarily convinced me that I had a great mix going... cheap boxed wine and Black Beauties. My routine built around my daily combo dose of courage and skinny, without any trips to the gym. No, something else broke through for just a moment.

Questions for you...

Think about a moment in your life when a light went on, an 'a-ha' moment that woke you up.

What happened?

What did you do with it?

*I distrust those people who know so well what God
wants, because I notice it always coincides
with their own desires.*
-Susan B. Anthony

Chapter 9

Forty-five Years Later...
A New Address

I am writing this piece on April 1, 2014. Today is my 30th anniversary of sobriety. I am sitting in my car which is parked in a residential-sticker-only parking spot at the North Hampton, NH State Beach. I am a five-minute drive from my house. I have authored one book, NOT LIKE MY MOTHER (had to plug it), and I am halfway through the book you are now reading. I am a 90-minute drive from Roxbury, Massachusetts, just 90 minutes by car from my throw-the black-beauties-in-the-toilet-bubble-bath chapter of my life. A car ride is one way to measure the distance; forty-five years of life between then and now is another.

So, what happened between the bathtub scene and April 1, 2014? I guess you can say a lifetime happened. A story unfolded.

I met my husband David in the summer of 1970. We met in my kitchen. David was in his last year of seminary and participating in a summer chaplaincy internship program at Mass General Hospital where my friend Lisa was working as secretary to the head chaplain. There she met and became friends with David. Lisa was living with me that summer. She invited David over to the apartment. He and I began a conversation which has never ended. It is now 47 years later.

David was earning his masters at Colgate Rochester Divinity School in Rochester, NY. At the time C.R.D.S was liberal and many of the clergy and students were deeply involved in the anti-war movement. Nightly, Walter Cronkite was on the evening news showing the numbers of American casualties from the war. Our troops, the Viet Cong, as well as civilians were being slaughtered. People everywhere were debating the justification of the war. From their pulpits clergy of diverse faiths were speaking in favor of or against the war. I was fascinated with David's courses. He was the only person I knew who went to graduate school. I asked question after question. David was a patient teacher. Today he says, "Irene was much more interested in my academics than I was." He sells himself short, he taught me plenty.

What were we doing in Vietnam? What were our moral and ethical responsibilities as the citizens whose tax dollars were supporting that war? It was a conversation and often an argument that was happening across the country at dinner tables, in coffee shops, in barrooms everywhere. Religion and politics were enameled together. They couldn't be separated. Love thy neighbor as thy self. Jesus taught peace and love. But the Bible said, "An eye for an eye..."

David and I talked for hours. Our conversations were my vicarious way of being on a college campus, not just being a part-time commuter student. Time with David made me feel a part of the movement. Also, David played the guitar and piano. I had sung in choir all through high school. He was *strumming me softly with his song*, as we filled my kitchen with hours of duets.

When David and I met he had finished his undergraduate degree from Syracuse University and upon graduation went directly to grad school. He then extended his grad school experience by one year with an internship program at Cornell University. There he served as a campus chaplain. These were dynamic times in the late 60's and early 70's. Schools like Cornell and Syracuse were filled with bright, able-bodied students whose whole male population was eligible for the draft and the war as soon as they graduated.

Everyone had a stake in the war in the 60's and 70's. We all knew someone who was serving or about to serve or hiding out in Canada because they refused to serve. Politicians used God's name regularly to justify what looked more and more like an unjustifiable mess.

God Bless our troops. The message was and still is—we are a Christian nation. The enemy is always a non-Christian nation. North Vietnamese were communists. Communists are not Christian. The government and military insisted we were in Vietnam to stop the spread of communism. Implicit was the message that to stop communism was protecting Christianity. God appears to be on our side.

More and more clergy were not having it. How was this slaughter of humanity God's plan? Who was this God that wanted us in a no-win war? Was unwillingness to fight in this war, cowardly or smart or brave? What was it? To picket and protest, to argue with authority...was this wrong? Was this sinful? Honor thy father and mother? Trust the church? Listen to the priests? Salute your flag? We are one nation under God. Ours is the only God nation—the one nation?

Nothing was black and white anymore. What did I believe? I believed my daughters needed a church. I had no idea how to raise children without a church, especially in the turbulent times we were living. So I took them to the closest Episcopal Church which was African-American. There we were in the minority. I have a faded Polaroid of the girls at 4 and 5. One is decorated in angel wings and a halo (a coat hanger wrapped in garland); the other in a white sheet tied with cord around her waist and a purple shawl covering her red hair. One was the angel and the other was Jesus' mom, Mary. Both are surrounded by beautiful African-American shepherds, wise men and a Joseph. I love the picture.

My new religious world was opened wider for me by Rev. Donofrio, the priest at the Roxbury church. As I said earlier, Episcopal ministers wear collars similar to their Catholic counterparts and are called priests. Pretty much the resemblance ends there. The theology has many differences. One biggie is Episcopal clergy are allowed to marry. Many Episcopalians when choosing a church prefer the pastor to be married. The sermons delivered by Father Donofrio were different than any Catholic priest I had ever experienced. He lived a completely different life than his Catholic counterparts. If you have a woman living with you, telling you to pick up your dirty towel from the bathroom floor and reminding you to take out the garbage; or you have watched your children cry with a broken heart for not being invited to a birthday party, then you see the world differently than a single man who is waited on by a paid housekeeper.

My favorite sermon, and a thought that has stayed with me, was a talk Father D. gave one Easter Sunday. He reminded us that the point of the Easter celebration wasn't about the crucifixion but was about the resurrection. The message was and is about eternal life... new beginnings... transformation. He spoke of how many Christians were hung up on the cross and didn't move onto the rebirth, the resurrection. Even the label of Christian was different. As a Catholic girl I knew we were called Catholics; all the other Christian churches were called Protestants. Later when the evangelical movement took off and mega-churches became common, churches began hiring marketing and branding consultants. No one said *Protestants* anymore. Today *Christian* is the in-name with churches, and many are debating which branch is *the most Christian.*

Gallons of Chianti and sangria later, Lisa moved out and basically David moved in. We were married the summer of 1971, and the girls and I moved to Rochester, NY once David graduated. He took on his first ministerial position in Penfield, NY. I was now the preacher's wife. Quite a turn of events for a divorced Catholic girl, who before the age of 16 thought it was a mortal sin to enter a Protestant church. She now committed a transgression right up there with having a hamburger on Friday with Satan himself.

I had to leave my little Episcopal church in Roxbury when I married David. David graduated C.R.D.S. and became an ordained American Baptist minister. His first job was as the assistant minister of the First Baptist Church of Penfield, NY. The girls and I were off on yet another adventure. (The American Baptist Church is not to be confused with the conservative Southern Baptist denomination. American Baptists are socially more liberal and very committed to being the "hands of Jesus" as they are all about service.)

That was the beginning of me as the minister's wife. I was a long way from a single divorced mom in white go-go boots running the streets of Boston "scooping" guys with my girlfriends. David and I are still talking about God, religion, ethics and politics. Now the difference is we are drinking herbal tea and going to bed a hell of a lot earlier.

Questions for you...

How has your religious or spiritual story unfolded?

What have been the questions you have asked?

What beliefs have been challenged?

When you are traveling at the speed of LIFE
we are bound to collide with each other.
-Paul Haggish-

Chapter 10

An Assistant Minister's Wife

Being an assistant minister's wife was a full-time job, a learning experience of disappointment and surprise. Often it was a point of contention between David and me.

David had no real passion for what he was doing. His first choice after college would have been to get experience in the working world. Enrolling in seminary was much more about what he *didn't* want to do. He did not want to get drafted into the military and go to Vietnam. At the time, the government offered seminarians an exemption from the draft. He had a strategy, not a calling.

Throughout my Catholic childhood, I was taught priests were called to their vocation. I was convinced men like Jesus, St. Francis or our local priests had been scouted out. I wasn't quite sure how that worked... in their sleep or what? But regardless of how they were notified–they knew. They had no doubt or question. They may have endured a wave of not being worthy, but they answered the call. It must have been something like, "You are one of the chosen ones–get suited up. Our people will be bringing the paperwork by in the morning."

Of course the females destined for the convent were called directly by the Blessed Virgin Mother herself. As the stories went she did not seem to have "people". She did all the contact work herself. I think mostly by appearing in visions. However it went, priests and nuns were touted by their superiors as having been called. They had *the* vocation.

David and his seminary grad school buddies never mentioned divine shoulder taps or celestial phone calls. Not once did I ever hear them use the word vocation. They used words like resumes, internships, career paths and job interviews.

Catholic clergy are assigned by their Bishops. Most Protestant clergy are hired through a typical job application process by their congregations.

Since I was not in Boston any longer and no one was getting memos from the Vatican, every point of reference I brought with me into my new religious world was no longer applicable. One glaring example of the different worlds was the Bible.

Being raised Catholic, I had no formal training or study of the Bible. I was taught that priests were the chosen ones with the power to read the Bible. It was their mandate to interpret it for us lay-people. It had been that way from the beginning. This was a major difference from the Protestant clergy. Non-Catholic clergy saw their charge to be teachers of the Bible, educating their congregations to read and study the Word. My husband and his friends all quoted the Bible and knew the stories by heart. They had grown up with it from their childhood Sunday school classes. In seminary they studied the Bible's origins. These young seminarians were being introduced for the first time to the political and social history that created the context from which the Biblical writings were created.

I was an adult before I realized there was anything more to the Bible than the gospel passages the priests read at Mass. Throughout my life, I have tried to love the Bible. I thought I should. I have tried even harder to like it. I don't. For me the Bible is like Steven King novels. I don't get what so many others see in them, with one exception—Steven's book, *ON WRITING*. I have read that one three times. Anyway, the Bible doesn't do it for me. I don't get it. I find the Bible boring and confusing, obtuse and annoying. I don't like how it is often produced with too much tiny print on weirdly thin paper.

Maybe I was in the 5th or 6th grade when we acquired our first home Bible. My introduction was a grand Catholic version that probably weighed ten pounds. Following Father Whoever's recommendation my mom (using rent money) bought this officially approved Catholic version of the King James Bible from the officially recommended door-to-door salesman. (This idea of selling Bibles for profit, and our being taught that only the priests could interpret the Word, was yet one more glaring contradiction that filled my religious instruction.)

Our shiny new family Bible came with a genuine embossed maroon leather cover and a thick grosgrain ribbon bookmark. The bookmark hung regally beyond the length of the book suspended from the lovely imitation mahogany book stand. It reminded me of a guest book at a funeral parlor.

My mom loved books. She didn't read them. She just loved them. She could read, however, focusing was difficult for her. She believed in education and the Catholic Church. Education would get her daughters out of poverty. The Church would get us all into heaven. Thus, the purchase of this holy book was for mom more important than rent. I opened it with the excitement I would open any new book. Initially, I found the size of the new tome both daunting and enticing... like the huge dictionary at the library whose size I found comforting. I figured that if a dictionary was that big it was guaranteed to have every word I could ever use. I assumed the same for the Bible. It must have all the rules that I would ever need.

I tried to read it. I couldn't. This Bible was not a children's version. It was the hard-core-unabridged-here's-what-2000-years-of-Catholic-doctrine-says version. I continued to rely on the priests' reading and re-reading the gospels from their pulpits. I followed along faithfully with my missal. I treated the priests the same way I treated my classroom teachers. They had gone to college. They had read the books. They knew the answers. I believed they knew what was best for me. They were the men of God. That is what they told me and what my mom believed. That Bible of ours, as far as I know, was never read by anyone. When mom died at age ninety no one wanted it.

In retrospect, it appears that my soul and the Universe conspired to shove my life forward by bringing me a Protestant minister to date and later marry. Don't you think it was a rather clever shove given how I stomped out of the Catholic Church?

Soul says, "Irene you are holding a red hot coal of anger

waiting to throw it at God. You have issues girlfriend. So I am going to put you right in the river of growth. Hang on my dear because there are churning rapids up ahead."

Questions for you...

A memoir is an autobiography with a theme.
A life theme does not usually take a straight line path.
However, it is often held together with a consistent thread.

What is a life theme of yours?

What thread is holding your theme together?

I thank thee, Father, Lord of heaven and earth, that
thou has hidden these things from
the wise and understanding
and revealed them to babies.
—Matthew 11:25

Chapter 11

Through Trial and Error

Learning to walk is an experience of trial and error motivated by an internal energy force. We push ourselves up. We fall and crawl and try again. We wobble and stand. We topple and stand again and again. But always the motivation, the impetus, comes from within. We persist some more. Up again, we totter... until that moment. That is the moment we realize the sensation of balance. The experience of balance now belongs to us. We have it. With our new discovery we can move, advance forward, backwards, sideways... all on our own.

Where did the impetus—the motivation to stand up, to walk—spring from? What is the Source of motivation? It is a force that pulses from within. Just what is it? Neither science nor religion can define it. No one can claim proof of its origin. Oh granted...some will argue it is electrical. Or some will call it nature or God. They will identify some of its properties. Ok, but where did it begin? Where is the Source? I certainly don't know what to call it. However, I do know that as young babies we hadn't yet learned to squash the energy. We hadn't yet learned to judge it. As babies we allowed it to be.

The baby is not thinking or saying, "Who do you think you are missy? Don't start standing up and getting all high and mighty. What if you do it wrong? What will people think?" We just flippin' do it. Undaunted we give it our best shot. We feel the urge and we go where it is taking us. We let it propel us. And we grin widely when we arrive at the balance and when the ability to walk is ours. We listen to ourselves. We hear what our being is calling us to do, and we surrender to the call. We *become* the walking and the running and the leaping and the dancing. The energy is our gift, then our skill and then our being...assimilated into our presence. Jesus says in the gospel, "... You must become as little children in order to enter the kingdom of heaven."

What if the Kingdom of Heaven is knowing without a doubt that you are a child of a most loving benevolent energy, a force that is on your side? And what if this energy flowed through you and as you from your very beginning? And what if the way the energy communicated with you was through your intuition?...your KNOWING?

I was born like every other child—in touch with my core, my Source. I followed the signals whatever they were. I learned to walk. Mom said I walked early. I also followed the impetus to sit up and roll over and make sounds and cry. I did what other babies and toddlers do. I listened to the directions from somewhere inside of me.

What happened? How did I lose connection? How do

any of us lose our contact to our inner guidance? Why do we start questioning and doubting ourselves until we can no longer hear our own inner voice or trust what we KNOW?

Pia Mellody explains it well in her book *Facing Co-dependence.* She describes how all children are born with five characteristics. Each child is naturally born valuable, vulnerable, needy and dependent, immature, and imperfect. When these characteristics are not honored, a child learns to squash them, thus diminishing themselves. For example, from a very young age I realized that my mom was in way over her head. My dad had left, never to return. Mom was carrying so much pain from her childhood that she was unable to be the adult her children needed. As the oldest, I was given responsibilities beyond my years. I was what psychologists label a "parentified" child. This means that I was often the acting-responsible adult in the family. My VULNERABILITY, NEEDS, DEPENDENCY, and IMMATURITY were not honored. In fact, they were completely ignored.

Involuntarily the child disconnects to not feel the pain. The pain in this example is fear. A child does not want to live in a world where her caregivers are not able to function. To survive, nature has given us denial. Denial is meant to be temporary. The problem for many is that survival and denial become our norm. To survive... to do what was asked of me... to be a good daughter... as the Bible says, "Honor thy mother and father"... I had to disconnect from my needs and wants. I had to show up for others. How does a child do that? Well, she subconsciously tells herself that she has no needs. She stops listening to her inner voice and guidance. She does it so much she believes her denial to be fact.

When we squash our needs and desires we shut off our connection to the main source of our individuality. We pay a big price to disconnect. We fill up with lots of judgment of ourselves and others. We have little sense of our purpose, our gifts and talents. We must put walls around our hearts. These walls keep us separate and often isolate us from love. We have difficulty in relationships. Our expectations of ourselves and others can be way out of whack. All of this leaves us with a deep-rooted sense of inadequacy.

Adaptations to our pain become our norm. The adaptive behavior becomes our default. We come to believe this default as fact. We accept a much lesser version of ourselves. Healing is about remembering the light that is our essence. We come back to the value of our preciousness.

Questions for you...

Clues to what we have buried in our subconscious often come in the form of desires.

Ask yourself... If I had no fear and money were no problem what would be fun to try?

What would be interesting to explore?

What do I say I will do when I retire? If I had time I would.... what?

Notice if you have any resistance to even exploring your desires. Is there a inner critic grumbling, "You are too old, not good enough?"

Just notice.
These are all beliefs. Are they your beliefs? Did they originate with someone else and do you still want them?

Owning our story and loving ourselves through the process
is the bravest thing we will ever do.
                                                    -Brene' Brown-

Chapter 12

A Program of Honesty

In 1983, I joined a program to look at overeating. At the time I was discouraged by my weight gain. I kept putting on the pounds. I was convinced I had a calorie problem. Surely if I just ate less my life would be perfect-because every woman thinks that if she is fitting into her skinny jeans her life will be flawless. This is how women think until they are fitting in their skinny jeans and life is still sucking. A friend of mine lost 50 pounds using a 12-Step program. I assumed it was the latest diet plan. And she said it was free to boot. Well alrighty then! Off I went. I had no idea my decision to attend her meeting would completely change my life.

My life on the outside looked good. On the inside I was crumbling. Like the song says... *"Is that all there is?"* I had achieved all the goals I had set for myself. I was a college graduate. I had an okay marriage. I loved my job. The girls were in college. I owned my own home (well, my husband, me and the bank). My car was reliable. Bills were paid. The refrigerator was full.

The 12-Step program opened my eyes. It gave me a

different perspective for pretty much everything I thought I knew about myself. Miracles have been defined as seeing the familiar through new lenses. My lenses were changing. For the first time I realized that I had God and the Catholic Church, or all religion for that matter, mushed into one. Like an egg in a cake, the ingredients couldn't be separated.

And remember, from the time I was 18 and married to Kevin, my definition of an alcoholic had been *him.* I pointed the finger at his drinking. He blacked out, didn't pay bills, lost his job and had DWIs, all under the influence of alcohol. I, on the other self-righteous hand, did not abandon the girls, paid bills, and had a good driving record... blah, blah, blah. What opened my eyes were the stories women in the food program shared. Many of the participants were also in a 12-Step program for their alcohol abuse. When I heard my new friends tell their stories, I heard my story. My denial was slowly being busted. The relationship women have with alcohol and drugs is often quite different than what men experience.

At the time, I was an executive director of a non-profit youth agency. I had been in the position for about 4 years. My team and I had just pulled off a coup. We sold a kindergarten program to our national organization and they were now in a contract to pay our agency a hefty quarterly sum for the next few years. In the non-profit world this does not happen. You can compare it to having the IRS buy a software program from you. Instead of you sending them a check yearly, they send you one. Obviously, this isn't the ordinary part of my story. The predictable piece is the way I drank while at the headquarters in Kansas City.

I stayed in a fun hotel which provided an open bar for

happy-hour every afternoon from 4–5 pm. I was there for 10 days. After 5 each evening I was treated to dinner and drinks. The national office had me in Kansas City to train volunteers from all over the country to implement the new program. I was like a large fish in a small pond.

At the end of my KC adventure I arrived back home in Massachusetts tired and disappointed with myself. For the previous eight months prior to the trip I had been following a food plan. Alcohol was not "allowed" on the plan. I was down 38 pounds. I felt good in clothes again. My thinking was clearer. I was more alive.

Prior to the food program, drinking was a part of everything we did as a couple: holidays, weekends, boating, birthdays, dinners out, business meetings, luncheons. Who knew you could eat pizza without a beer? Then there was morning drinking on special occasions... it was called brunch. The "special" occasion had become more frequent and the "weekends" were starting earlier in the week. Listening week after week to the food program participants share their experience with alcohol, I began to seriously look at mine. I knew all too well what they were talking about.

One way we stay stuck in old behavior that does not serve us is to compare ourselves to others. Making Kevin my definition of an alcoholic was an effective diversion for me. With resolute disdain in my heart, I held him as the poster face of alcoholism. Myself, I held on a raised platform of martyrdom. Look at me. As a single mom I kept the girls fed, housed, and clothed with no help from him. I paid the bills. I bettered myself with a college education. How could I be an alcoholic? No! He was the loser.

Now, as a remarried mother, I was identifying with

women calling themselves alcoholics. Before my eight-month hiatus I often drank more than I planned. Many times I drove a car when I had to shut one eye not to see double. I'd thrown up in toilets till I had the dry heaves; spent many a morning drinking orange juice and coffee trying to get my head clear before going to work. I could be irritable and impossible to please. I was hard on my daughters and harder on my husband. Repeatedly I would promise myself to cool it. Repeatedly I drank more than I planned. It wasn't a game anymore. More than I wanted to acknowledge, alcohol was choosing me without my permission. All our friends drank. It was part of the fabric of our social life.

Only once did a red flag momentarily penetrate my denial. David and I were getting behind financially. Often we did not have enough money to make it through the month. Both of us were working full-time in human services... not big paying jobs but decent. And yet we constantly had more month than money. I made an appointment with a financial planner. He was an acquaintance and we liked him well enough. It wasn't easy for either of us to let ourselves be vulnerable and transparent, but we did it. He gave us some homework. We were to get little spiral notebooks, and each keep a record of every penny we spent for the next 30 days. Then we were to divide the tracking into categories, one being food. When we ate out we had to divide that expense into food or alcohol, not just food. The instructions were that we not change the way we spent, just track it.

Off we went. We diligently stuck to the plan and tracked every dime we spent. When we got to the end of the month we added our columns and were really uncomfortable when we saw how much money we were spending on alcohol. Our monthly expense for beverages was an eye opener. Thus we did what good functioning alcoholics would do, we quickly agreed that given our budget we couldn't afford the financial planner.

From this rearview mirror 30 years later, I realize that it was me, myself, the great Irene, who didn't want to own the truth. I was humiliated. I was afraid. Alcohol had become my God. I relied on it. It was what I counted on. It was the anesthesia—a numbing agent that kept me from feeling. I needed something, or a couple of some things to keep my uncomfortable feelings squashed. Unconsciously I used alcohol, food and work to dull my feelings. Keep me busy, busy, busy. Me...sit still or breathe in deeply, pause and reflect? Oh no, not moi. No way would I open access to feelings. I wanted control. Sub-consciously my goal was to be numb. Staying in my head was my default. Living out of touch with my being was like using my right hand. It was what I knew with no idea when or how I learned it. I judged anyone who talked about their difficult feelings as annoying whiners with an attitude problem. "Stop with the drama," was my judgment! If I wouldn't let me have my feelings, I couldn't let you have yours!

When I slammed the door on the Catholic Church, I slammed the door on God. In the first 12-Step fellowship I joined, I was confronted with the idea that on my own, my life wasn't working. I needed the help of a power greater than myself. It was up to me to define what higher power meant to me. Some people in the group believed it was the power of the group itself. Some had no problem naming it God. Many were atheists or agnostics. Me, I believed in God. I always had. My issue...I was pissed at the big G with absolutely no intention whatsoever of relying on the #@$%^ ever again. Doing business with God meant following rules set down by someone else–usually some man.

My attitude, fueled by anger, was being challenged. For eight months I had been listening to women (and some men) who couldn't control their eating, and many their drinking. The only thing that helped them was to surrender to a power greater than themselves. Oh yay. Slowly, I was beginning to trust what I witnessed in the food program. I watched others change for the better. I had realized some success for 8 months. I experienced a bit of relief. The success was no compulsive eating or drinking. I felt good. I lost weight. I didn't have temper outbursts. I carried a new calm about myself that was comforting.

With only a few months of living the new life style, like I said earlier, I found myself in Kansas City, all-expenses paid. The first night while out for dinner I decided a beer would go great with what I ordered. Then it was a second beer, and why not a cigarette? Here I was again. I didn't get drunk that night. But it would only be a matter of time. I would be right back where I started the year earlier. The eight months without drinking had given me enough clarity to recognize that my primary problem was not the food. It was my relationship with alcohol. On my own I wasn't capable of doing what I needed to do. I needed help. I found another 12-Step program only this time it dealt with alcohol. I have been in that program now for over 30 years.

So why do I want to share with you the story of my coming to terms with my abuse of alcohol? What connection is there to my spiritual journey? Or more importantly, what relevance does this have to yours? Drinking or not drinking alcohol is not the point. I totally get that you may not relate to my whole alcohol issue. But I am guessing that there are other ways you have made something in your life your *"God."* You rely on something or someone outside of yourself to make life more tolerable. You put your trust in something that you imagine keeps you safe or life bearable. It could be prescription drugs, your savings account, a partner, your looks, your clothes, spending, gambling, your job etc. You know the deal. What do you believe you can't live without?

I put alcohol down. Down means *nothing*! Nothing means no little sips, no special occasion drinks, no toasts at a wedding... naddah. Without alcohol I was confronted with how filled I was with fear. All my adult life I believed I was a tough broad. I had no compassion or respect for vulnerability. I also had no clue that I kept myself diverted from difficult feelings with busyness, alcohol and blaming. Without alcohol I experienced anxiety attacks for the first time. It is an understatement to say I was uncomfortable in my own skin.

I knew that there was no way around what I was experiencing. I had to go through it. As I learned to be with the feelings, I knew I was on the right path. It was time to meet myself in a way I had never experienced. The KNOWING was an intuition... an awareness that I was no longer ignoring.

KNOWING is not intelligence. It is not logic. It is the quiet persistent voice from below your heart softly whispering TRUTH. Whispering my TRUTH, whispering YOUR TRUTH, it is that voice of guidance telling you what you often don't want to hear. If we listen we will lose our routine, our way of being. Our familiar will be flipped over. Often the KNOWING opens new doors. Doors opening to paths we have been afraid to walk. My little voice had been telling me for years, "Irene you have a problem with alcohol." I didn't want the heads up. I wanted to be normal. I wanted to be like everyone else. I wanted to keep doing what I believed worked for me. I wanted to keep the familiar.

Questions for you...

In the quiet of your being what do you hear?

Does it scare you?

Does it call you to an action you may be afraid to take?

Before the truth can set you free
find out what lies have been holding you hostage.
-unknown-

Chapter 13

Not On My Knees

On my side of the bed, I was lying on my back staring at God. Well, God in the form of my bedroom ceiling. David was asleep. I was touching his right arm with my left hand. My new sponsor (a mentor in my 12-Step program) had given me a suggestion. Her job was to share with me what she had done to keep sober. She was a woman a bit older than me, who had a whole lot more 24 hours of not drinking. She was suggesting I might want to imitate her nightly routine. She got on her knees beside her bed and thanked a power greater than herself for her day of sobriety. In the morning the first thing she did was again return to her knees and ask this same "power" for another 24 hours without a drink of alcohol. The purpose wasn't to worship some invisible deity, but rather a humbling of her ego... a gesture of surrender, an expression of recognition to a bigger energy of *Something,* that is working with and through us. This routine was working for her. And from what I was hearing it was also helping thousands of others through the program world-wide.

I had no problem with the gratitude. I was experiencing the impossible. I was more than 30 days sober. I had not had one drop of alcohol in a little more than four weeks....4 weekends...without any kind of booze...nothing whatsoever. For years weekends were my downfall. Honestly, they were beginning on Wednesday nights. Over and again I broke promises to myself swearing that I would not drink. I had become just like my father who promised to not take the rent money to the track; like my ex-husband who swore he was done with drinking and driving; like the army of human beings before me who swore "no more!" No more doing what was ruining health, relationships, and peace. One thing I had in common with the people I judged so harshly was a collection of my own failed promises. Each promise was met with another excuse why this time would be different. Why this time I deserved just one more glass of wine.

Now I had four weeks sober which included four weekends... back to back. The evil spell had been broken. I had found a wave of something that was working. I was surprised and grateful. The fog of pre-occupation with drinking or not drinking was lifted. I KNEW something more than sheer will was working this new miracle for and through me. Whatever it was... the group energy of the program, my sponsor, or some combination of the stories the group members shared, a new wind had lifted my sails. I was experiencing a ride of freedom that was delicious. Oh yes, I was grateful. I was beginning to use the term *Higher Power.* Just don't ask me to call it GOD. Even less, do not imagine I am getting on my knees, ever again, to talk to this *Something*...no flipping way in hell.

I lay in bed with my fists curled tight, my legs taut and my teeth clenched as I thanked my ceiling. My back was rigid with resolve. Fool me once, shame on you. Fool me twice, shame on me. At the age of twelve I gave *You* my heart, my innocence and my trust. I loved the comfort of slipping into a pew and dropping the kneeler to the floor. I remember moving my knees to the vinyl padding while I made *Your* sign of the cross with my right hand. I crossed my hand from forehead to heart and left shoulder to right shoulder a thousand times. This ritual was as familiar and comforting as crawling into bed, pulling clean sheets and a warm blanket up to my face. Every conversation with *You*, God, before I was 20 began by drawing *Your* son's cross on my chest. How often was I on my knees? I trusted *You* like I now trust my favorite cup of tea and honey. But *Your* cup shattered and my whole life was scalded with the mess. The tension in my body reminded me of the betrayal. My mind stayed on red alert for fight or flight, while my heart was beginning to soften. This is what gratitude does. It softens. It doesn't listen to the mind. It enters through the experience of the heart. It remembers the Truth. Truth comes through Divine Grace.

This surrender was the opening of a new consciousness. I was beginning to drop the rocks of rage and disappointment. These heavy rocks with their jagged edges were cutting into my peace, and for the first time I was noticing.

Questions for you...

***Does your heart need to soften about something?
What stops you?***

Knowing yourself is the beginning of wisdom.
-Aristotle-

Chapter 14

The Produce Aisle

I was sitting in the parking lot of Hannaford's Supermarket, a place I had probably been a hundred times before. On this particular Saturday afternoon, however, it was as if I had arrived on a new planet. The parking lot looked the same with metal carriages, mini-vans showing off New Hampshire license plates, Easter lilies stacked outside ready for purchase; all was the same.

It was April 1, 1989 about 4:00 in the afternoon. I had left the house at 8:00 A.M. a few minutes behind David, and I would be out for the day. He would be gone for 6 months. I celebrated my fifth year of sobriety that morning at a 12-Step meeting followed by lunch with friends and some fun hanging out. My new thick brass 5-year medallion was tucked in the side pocket of my purse.

Everything was as the day before. The palpable difference on April 1, 1989 was me. I was 43 years old, and this was the first day in my entire life that I was living alone. I was going home to an empty house. David had left early that morning for a 10-hour drive to Wernersville, PA where he would begin a residential internship program at the Caron Institute. His goal was to gain a certification as an expressive therapist/specialist in the field of Adult Children of Alcoholics.

At this point in our story, David was 3 years sober. After watching me look at my relationship with alcohol, he began to look at his. He then joined the 12 Step path. Our program describes itself as a "program of honesty." The honesty it refers to is honesty with ourselves. The previous five years had opened us up to look in the dark corners of our history and behaviors. We looked at places where we had never before shined any light. It was a rich time of owning our personal histories and taking inventory of our past. Through the process, David felt called to use his pastoral education in counseling and make a change in his career path. He decided to go into private practice as a counselor. This internship in Pennsylvania was the training he needed.

I supported him in his decision. We cashed in a little retirement fund which, when added to a small stipend he would receive and my full-time job in corporate human resources, gave us enough temporary financial leeway. This was a big change for us as a couple. It turned out to be an even bigger change for me individually.

So… let's go back to the grocery store.

I walked in through the automatic doors pushing my cart. This routine is about as ordinary as it gets. Once inside, just past the bakery and smack in the middle of the produce aisle, I froze. It wasn't a panic. I didn't have an anxiety attack. I simply froze. I did not know what to do or where to go. I had zero clues. No point of reference. What did I want? I knew how to plan dinners for my family, my husband, my guests, and somebody other than me. I had never gone into a grocery store with only myself to think about. This realization was stunning. I wanted to stop someone, anyone, and say, "Can you help me? I am having a special moment here. I don't know whether to add this to my baby book as a first, or to cry. I don't think I ever received the memo of how to buy groceries for the week for one person, especially if that one person is me."

I walked up and down the aisles. I read labels. I was too blank to even criticize myself. It was more like I was trying to start speaking Chinese without lessons. I had no point of reference. I didn't know what I wanted. Literally 45 minutes later, I ended up at the magazine rack. I flipped through the periodicals like a space alien trying to figure out where I had landed.

Another 45 minutes later, without anyone calling the medics, I cashed out. I bought a yogurt and a People magazine. That was the beginning of my awakening consciousness; my first steps on the journey that would take me back to my Self. Ok, let me get real... it was less like a journey and better defined as a "schlep."

Back in the driver's seat of my car, the mental fog lifted and revealed (with no cushion of denial) how much I had been hiding out in the land of alcohol and co-dependency. I was in a program that preached the "gospel" of personal honesty. To be honest with myself, I first had to have a Self.

Questions for you...

Humans appear to be divided into two groups:
Those who focus primarily on others and lose themselves...

Or those focused mostly on themselves and lose connection
to others.
What is your proclivity?

Step 11
"Sought through prayer and meditation to improve our conscious contact with God as we understood Him, praying only for knowledge of His will for us and the power to carry that out."
-The Big Book of Alcoholics Anonymous-

Chapter 15

Racing to Meditation

Joining the 12-Step world of meetings and support changed my life completely.

My sponsor, Kathy, was on the phone asking me, *"Irene have you meditated yet today?"* I remember it like it was yesterday. I have told this story many times.

I squeezed my head more to the left as I lifted my shoulder higher pinching the black receiver tighter to my ear. I ignored the stiffness that was forming in my right shoulder. My body was losing patience with my awkward position. Speaker phones hadn't yet been invented. Multitasking in 1984 took a bit more physicality.

I replied proudly, *"Yes, I am sitting quietly. I just turned off the T.V. and I have my cup of tea. I am knitting, and I have my Big Book perched here in front of me. I feel great. No cigarettes and everything is quiet. Just me knitting and the Big Book. I am going to give it 20 more minutes. How's that?"*

"Well, dear, that's not meditating. The 11th step says prayer and meditation to improve our conscious contact with a power greater than ourselves. Not take some time to work on making

Christmas presents. What I want you to do is finish your cup of tea. Close the book. Put your knitting down and do nothing for one minute... 60 seconds. Just close your eyes and breathe."

Everything in me pushed back. A tsunami of resistance wanted to tell Kathy, of course in the most loving way, to FUCK OFF. Did she not get how much I had to do? I was one very productive busy woman. Because I had not had alcohol for almost a year I was able to control my tongue. No simple achievement for me.

"Kathy, I don't have time for that."

"Irene, can you hear yourself? I asked you to sit and breathe with your eyes closed for 60 seconds. Jesus Christ took time out of his schedule to do it for 40 days. My guess is you can do it for 60 seconds."

"Kathy, have I ever told you how much I hate you, especially when you are right? Ugh... ok... ok."

"Love you too, Irene. So…call me back after your one minute is done."

With the attitude of a 13-year-old going into time out, I put down my knitting and hung up the receiver. My neck and shoulder were pleased. My hands missed the busyness of slipping the needles through the yarn. That is where I first felt the nudginess. Then my stomach tightened. I looked at the clock. I decided to wait for the second hand to reach the 12. I closed my eyes. My breathing was shallow. I noticed tightness in my upper chest, just below my throat. I couldn't get a deep easy breath. I opened my eyes. Ten seconds had passed. *Shit are you kidding me?! I am going to suffocate.* I closed my eyes again. Cravings began to surface, wiggling up from under my rib cage and moving towards my brain. *Toast would be good...a grilled cheese sandwich even better.*

Oh yeah, I've got leftover cheddar cheese. Now I'm talking..a big slice of tomato in between the cheese slices and bread. Yah baby! Breathe Irene. I looked at the clock.

Twenty seconds... 20 seconds! I was outraged—no, I was scared. I couldn't breathe. I couldn't get the air to go past the pressure in my chest.

Again I closed my eyes, remembering what I had heard at meetings. "Are you willing to go to any length?" *Why is this so hard for me?* I had to put my hands under my butt. I was forcing myself to sit still. I was 38 years old and I could not sit still for 60 seconds. *Don't ask me to sit. Give me work to do! I dared look at the clock again.* 35 seconds had crawled by. *Oh sweet Jezusss will this ever end? This is a lot like labor without the sweat, and no one is giving me ice to chew on!*

Determined, I closed my eyes again. I began to focus on my breathing. It was simultaneously scaring me and frustrating me. I could not get a deep breath. How long had this been going on? Somehow it felt familiar, though I am not sure that I ever noticed it before. Who was I kidding? I had never paused to take notice. Observing my breathing was a new neighborhood for me to explore.

How could I be 38 years old and not know what my breathing was doing? That was my first official "aha" meditation moment. I was taking the first steps to waking up.

I looked at the clock. Sixty-eight seconds had passed. I did it!

Learning to be with stillness.

Questions for you...

This cairn has changed my life for the better in too many ways to count. If you haven't already included stillness in your daily life, do it now. Just stop reading for sixty seconds. Breathe and close your eyes.
If you resist, notice why.

Check out what is going on inside of you when you think about doing 60 seconds of stillness.

If you didn't do it, I am gonna' ask...what are you afraid of?
No... blah, blah, blah... the only reason you don't stop for one moment of stillness is your fear of being with YOU.

Our own life is the instrument
with which we experiment with truth.
Thich Nhat Hanh

Chapter 16

I'm A Therapist?

Every weekend for the six months David was away doing his internship we would drive four hours toward each other. On Friday nights we met halfway between Pennsylvania and New Hampshire at a campground in Red Hook, NY. This beautiful town of rolling hills on the Hudson River became our weekly hideaway. Our first weekend in April the jug of water we had on the picnic table froze. The last weekend was the end of September when the leaves were golden and farm stands were selling apples.

In our little Ford van these weekends were a mixed emotional experience. They were fun and romantic, painful and healing. For the first time in eighteen years we were alone with no young family obligations. Remember, our coupleship began with two children.

During these six months there were many firsts. I was adapting easily (too easily) to living alone, while David was digging deep into his family of origin emotional history. The educational twist when studying to be a therapist is that you set out to be a healer for others and end up looking at your own pain. Therapists can't take a client to places they themselves are not willing to go. If a counselor has not owned his/her anger, fear, grief and pain, they cannot lead clients through theirs.

Six months of the internship training at the Caron Foundation brought David face-to-face with his traumatic childhood issues. Every week more and more layers of his story were revealed. He learned what happened, how it landed and how he adapted to survive. While identifying his long-held beliefs about himself and his family, David was learning how those beliefs were running his life without his permission. He was gaining clarity for how embedded his old beliefs were in his psyche.

Friday nights we arrived at the campsite tired from our long drives and very full weeks. We were also excited to share our overflowing insights. While David was beating his new found rage out on therapeutic pillows, I was taking a meditation class and reading Wayne Dyer and Gerald Jampolsky. Simultaneously, life at my job was changing. At this time I was working in corporate America and with it came a new office and secretary. At the same time I was being recruited by another company. Life was positive. I found myself beginning to fill David's side of the closet with my clothes and spread out in our bed with my books and pillows. I no longer had difficulty at the grocery store and enjoyed not having to compromise my selections at the video store (This was 1989. The wheel had been invented but there was no Netflix). We were changing, and our marriage had to keep up.

With David becoming more vulnerable while I was enjoying the freedom of a single lifestyle, our two worlds began to rub up against each other as the weeks passed. He felt abandoned by his partner. My world was humming. I had a great date every weekend, and no one to pick up after during the week. I was not the comforter for him I had always been, and he wasn't the fun guy who wanted to play with me. At the end of the six months, I attended Caron's week long in-patient program for co-dependency. I became the student for 6 days that David had been for 6 months. The experience forced me to examine my interior life which had never seen the light of day.

After eighteen years of marriage, like any couple, we had developed patterns of behavior that were not optimum, but were familiar. Now, we were both sober and raw. No more alcohol and no place to hide. This was us. We were completely naked to ourselves and exposed in our relationship. Everything was out in the open. Transparency was not an option; it had become a mandate.

Today we are approaching forty-seven years of marriage. People will often ask, "How did you do it?" I answer the more revealing question is not *how* we did it, but *why* did we do it? *How* we stayed together for forty-seven years is easy. No one left and no one died. *Why* we stayed is the harder question to answer. Couples have divorced for fewer reasons than we have had. Over the years we have hurt each other, betrayed each other and been mean to each other in all the ways couples can. I have been a screamer, he has been passive aggressive. We have been complete jerks to each other, AND we have chosen to stay. Why?

The WHY has to do with our spiritual beliefs. These beliefs are NOT religious. The late Scott Peck wrote a definition of love in his ground-breaking book, THE ROAD

LESS TRAVELED. He said, *"Love is the will to extend one's self for the purpose of nurturing one's own or another's spiritual growth."* And we believe that all growth is spiritual and is the primary purpose of marriage. Marriage challenges us to show up for the relationship without losing ourselves. Nothing has called me to deeper or more meaningful growth than my marriage.

Spirituality is your relationship with life. It is the path we explore to our deepest values and meaning by which we live. Fortunately, David and I have been willing to do the growing. Paleeeezzze do not think we skipped through the process singing Kumbaya. We were more like a reality TV show.

From the moment we met, we began a conversation about our beliefs and values. Today we are still in that conversation exploring them. We have fought over so many different stupid things. But there are two things which we have never disagreed; those are politics and our core spiritual values. Politics for us is the outward manifestation of how people take a stand for their core values.

We believe in a Higher Power and one of the many words we use to describe this power is LOVE. We believe that *IT* is the overriding force of all and it is benevolent. We believe that evil is fear, and from our fear, all human craziness stems. Fear such as: Y*ou are going to get what is mine...* pushes us to act on... *So I will get you first.* There are a zillion ways we humans express fear and a zillion more how we express love. And the choice is ours...we have free will.

I believe human beings are in some other realm before we arrive on planet earth, and there will be a different reality we will enter when we leave. In the meantime our unraveling stories in the present are just a few chapters in a much larger narrative.

To our intellects our earthly sagas often do not make sense or seem fair. I ultimately trust our stories are perfect for each of us, that we may learn what we need to learn. If we open to the lessons they serve us. The time will come when we will recognize the good. Life does not make sense nor is it fair. I don't believe fairness is the purpose. I believe my purpose is to remember the benevolent seeds of my beginning, and to remember that every other being on the planet has the same essence. Ok, often the behaviors of human beings do not look like they sprout from goodness. However, every brand new baby I have ever been around begs to differ. Infants show me from whence we all come. Their innocence and vulnerability, their vibration is pure. My earthly task is to remember I came from that same goodness. When I can be with myself with compassion, I behave in much more "Goodly" ways.

Ok, all well and good but how did I go from a campground in the Hudson Valley to a therapist in New Hampshire?

David came home from his internship fired up and ready to go. He set up a private counseling practice and to promote his work he offered educational retreat weekends. He solicited my input and help. My work in the corporate world was in employee education. Together we developed curriculum for his weekends. I then assisted him in the execution of the programs. To my surprise participants began to ask me if I would see them individually in David's office. From this beginning my private practice was born. From childhood I always knew I would work with children, hence the Early Childhood Education undergrad degree. Today, *I do work with children*. However, they are in *grown-up bodies*. What I am saying is I work with adults to help them come home to their childhood stories with compassion for themselves. I believe 99% of our issues stem from unresolved childhood stories. Often our lives are being directed by the defenses of our "inner child". Don't poo poo this until you have owned it.

Questions for you...

What is working in your life and you would not change it?

What is not working?

How is it not working? Is this a familiar scenario?

Have the circumstances changed but the feelings are familiar?
Just notice.

Your soul is the quiet voice inside of you
that tells you there is more.
-Rob Bell-

Chapter 17

Carrie

═══════════

Carrie was my friend. I am sure she still is. She died seven years ago. During the last eighteen months of her life she and I shared from a place of deep transparency. I was her 12-Step sponsor and she was the editor (also coach) for my first book. I was the person she called from the doctor's office to confirm that her persistent cough was indeed inoperable lung cancer. From that moment on we held each other's hand through the minefield of vulnerability. Carrie was an aggravating mix of self-centeredness and generosity; deep faith and scathing cynicism. She was brilliant and naive. She was fully human and often not of this world.

Carrie had admiration and respect for my work as a therapist. She often referred clients. I know she loved me by all the trust she gave me. Trust was a challenging gift for Carrie to offer.

I was familiar with the dying process. During my last year of graduate school, I interned with an inspiring hospice program in Manchester, NH. If any single experience in my life convinced me that there is another realm, an existence beyond this earthly one, it was hospice. Sharing the last week of Carrie's life was profound. Carrie's transition only cemented my KNOWING... knowing there are dimensions beyond this earthly one.

One of Carrie's favorite pastimes was reading. She absorbed books. She had her husband Michael build a sitting room that was filled with his hand-crafted wooden book shelves. In the room he created a classic window seat nestled in between the floor to ceiling shelves. It was perfectly wide enough that two could sit facing, both friends stretching their legs with the soles of their feet meeting. Carrie enjoyed sitting with her back against the frame, her lap under a beige crocheted afghan, reading and drinking coffee. She shared the space with her inner circle of girlfriends. She would tell us why we had to read whatever book she was excited about that week. Many of the books were about spirituality. She was ahead of the rest of us. She knew the cool stuff way before anyone–even Oprah.

One afternoon about four days before she transitioned I was sitting with her on her window seat. She loved holding court there. I would jerk her chain, teasing her that she was really born into the wrong era. She was better suited for a scene in a Masterpiece Theater production. Anyway, that afternoon she was alert and her pain had eased for a little. A conversation or questions were not an imposition for her. Anyone who has sat with a friend who is slowly leaving the planet knows how precious those last few conversations are. She was glad to be present, and I was pleased to have her attention. I don't know what provoked me but I asked, "Carrie, now that you are in the last chapter of this life, do you regret anything?" She looked at me seriously and replied, "I regret everything." Then with a smile she finished by saying, "And now I know none of it matters."

She explained that during the last two weeks she had been visiting the "other side." She said at first her "visits" felt like dreams, but then more and more she trusted what she was experiencing during her waking hours. She was surrendering to them. She described where she visited was nothing but light and pure love. She said when she was there, there was no history, no past, nothing but the present. Propelled by determination, with startling clarity, Carrie used every bit of strength she had to grab my attention and speak to me. She said, "Irene, I want you to get this. It is all LOVE. There is nothing else. It is a love I can't describe because it is different than any kind of love you or I have experienced on earth. I want you to know this. I know how many people you influence. I want you to know. Love is all there is."

The next afternoon Carrie gave me a second big conversation. It was my turn to take a shift of care-giving. She needed round the clock care. I was there to replace another of Carrie's close friends. We were helping Carrie make it to the bathroom. Everything in her body was releasing. We were trying to clean Carrie and give her dignity and honor. It was difficult. Cancer at the end is so damn blunt, nothing subtle. It sucked. Our dear Carrie looked at us, as we both lifted her frail body onto her bed. She said something to the effect that she felt bad for the fear and worry on our faces. She said, "I am not feeling the pain you guys are afraid of. I am not in this body. I am not here any longer." Those words were some of her last. They were the last ones that I heard. I was scheduled to leave for a trip the next day. She encouraged me to go. Carrie and I said goodbye. We knew it was our last time together in this realm. She died less than 36 hours later.

Carrie dug into the very marrow of her tired sick bones to hang on. I KNEW she had given me a valuable gift. At the time, I didn't understand what inestimable worth it held. Using her last wisps of life, she stayed in her body just a bit longer that I might hear what she was learning.

There were five women Carrie invited into her final circle. We each had our separate conversations with her. Since her passing we have all agreed those conversations blessed us beyond imagination. Carrie gave us a glimpse into the world toward which she was rapidly moving. We were grateful for the light she poured on her path. It wasn't until Anita Moorjani wrote *Dying To Be Me,* the blockbuster memoir of her near death experience, that I was able to appreciate what Carrie did for me.

Here is what I received. My KNOWING was validated by Carrie. I KNOW there is more than what we think and see here in this earthly reality. KNOWING is not from logic. KNOWING is from experience. KNOWING is a resonance, a vibration that brings your interior being into harmony. You experience a sweet spot, like hitting a perfect shot with a tennis racquet or golf club. It is finding the exact right color to paint your bedroom, or looking into the face of your new born child and KNOWING... ahhh yes, this baby is meant for me, or finding your furry soul mate at the SPCA kennel. KNOWING shares no space with doubt. It is clarity, a perfect fit. KNOWING is an experience of your authentic TRUTH. This is not the truth (small t) of being right...I am right you are wrong...let me prove it. This is not my ego out-debating your ego.

This is KNOWING, conscious intuition. It happens from your neck down. It does not happen in your head. It is satisfying with a quiet stillness. KNOWING is your TRUTH and it often comes in a whisper. Of course, you can and most likely will question your KNOWING. You will come up with a zillion reasons to not follow your KNOWING. What will people think? What if you are wrong? What if this is a mistake? Fear nags and nags. But your KNOWING persists. You cannot let it go. It feels right... for you.

Questions for you...

You listen. You trust.
We need to listen and trust what we KNOW.
It is our internal GPS. It is our guidance system and we
need to listen and then trust what we hear.

Why must we?

Well, tell me about a time in your life when you
recognized your KNOWING BUT didn't listen. How
did that work out?

We need to listen and trust because the guidance is ours.
It is specifically given to us.
It is the voice of our SOURCE.

*The reason people awaken is because
they have finally stopped agreeing to
things that insult their soul.*
- unknown-

Chapter 18

Puerto Vallarta, Mexico

I woke up before light in Puerto Vallarta, Mexico. The sky was black with few stars. The cool air reminded me how many light weight jackets I had at home, of course all of which I did not bring. Then she started, my inner critic (I call her Bitch-babe) *"Irene you should have packed better... more efficiently... you missed the mark."* There she was all warmed up, and the sun hadn't come up yet. Her critical observations have dulled the color of my life for as long as I have been able to pay attention to my thoughts. Wherever I am, wherever I go, whatever I am doing, there Bitch-babe is. She is turning down the color on my experience dial. *"Just not good enough Irene."* Bitch-babe has repeated this put-down 10,000 X 10,000 times during my lifetime.

Now before dawn, after a warm shower and some clean clothes, I was walking along the ocean's edge. I was exploring the Malecon (the city promenade) in the dark. I enjoyed being rested. It had been 24 hours of traveling the day before. There was enough activity stirring to make me feel safe. I felt secure and blessed to be right where I was.

My fantasy was to find the Starbucks I had seen from the taxi cab window the day before. No, not open until 8 am. I had a while before coffee and Wi-Fi. I walked. The sidewalk was steadily being populated with runners. Many looked to be my age. Puerto Vallarta holds a large community of retired Americans. Well, this morning quite a few of them were down here jogging. All the joggers were thin. It's funny how that works. You hardly ever see a chubby runner. These folks were the tuck-in-your-shirt kind of thin.

Here she goes. Bitch-babe starts. *"Look at you. There is no excuse for your weight."* I whine back. *"Well, I would run, too, every morning if it wasn't minus eight degrees back in New Hampshire."* She will have none of my excuses. *"Bundle up... or use a workout DVD... just move your ass."* Bitch-Babe never sleeps. She is like the energizer bunny but not as cute. She is sharpened and ready to cut into any balloon my experience is floating.

In a small well-lit alley-way, past a quiet gentle man sweeping yesterday's debris from the sidewalk, just beyond the handsome gray-haired guy setting up his bread cart, I climbed a steep cobblestone staircase guiding me to the town's large basilica. There, I am welcomed with two large wooden doors that are wide open. The doors seem to have been pushed open by the glorious light that is pouring out of the sanctuary. Inside the large stone church all the walls are painted a brilliant white. The walls display an abundance of art and color. No windows are closed, and the sanctuary is lit like an automobile showroom. Inviting and welcoming, it silently calls everyone to come in. *Hola, hello. Sientese, come sit down.*

I decide to spend the rest of my time waiting for

Starbucks to open by sitting in the church. I figure I will use the time to meditate and open to whatever memories reveal themselves. (I was in the middle of writing the book you are now reading.) Good idea. I am intrigued to be in a Mexican Catholic Church. I love the gold paint trimming the columns and molding that circled the inside walls. Folk art treatment of Renaissance motifs is everywhere. The energy of the sanctuary feels light because of the brightness. I am intrigued that the altar is not framing a thorned bloody Jesus on a cross, but rather a soft painting of his mother. Mary holds the place of honor. I am hopeful.

Then I slide into a pew. A pew designed by the same guy who patented the guillotine. I look around to see if I have chosen a broken pew. No. They are all the same... wooden slats spaced just far enough apart so as not to allow one body part any comfort. I carry a lot of padding. This guy had to go the extra mile to achieve my instant discomfort.

Ok. I bargain with myself. *Your discomfort is a small sacrifice to swap for an hour of insight. Just watch the parishioners. Sit still and breathe.* An elderly man walks in and kneels at the altar. He stays for 30 seconds and walks out a back door. A woman, probably my age dressed in Capri pants, moves past me down the aisle closer to the front. She slides into a pew with the confidence attached to a familiar routine. Without taking her eyes off the picture of Mary, she reaches into her pocketbook and takes out her rosary and begins to move her lips and rub her beads. I remembered the comfort of beads. Now my back is seizing. *Really, I am all set with this pew.*

Alright, I think, *Why not do the rest of your time on your knees. The kneeler is padded.*

"*Sit still.*" Bitch-babe snaps. "*Suck it up. You are being impatient. Now there's a surprise!*" (Bitch-babe can be snarky.)

Meanwhile, a woman with two boys, one maybe 14 or 15 and a younger one 6 or 7, walked past me. She finds a seat on the opposite side of the aisle. They are far enough in front of me to be clearly in my view. This woman using the touch of a protective angel puts her hand on the younger boy's back. She guides him to kneel beside her. The older boy watches and follows. She takes the hand of the little guy, while he kneels beside her and gently moves it across his chest, teaching him how to make the sign of the cross. I figure these kids are not her biological sons. I am thinking if this religiously enthusiastic woman had given birth to these two boys, they would definitely know how to make a sign of the cross at their ages. The older boy watches and again follows her lead. Each boy looks at her with eyes of appreciation. They want to know. They want to do it right. They want to do what will please her.

I remember being little and wanting to know. *Show me. Tell me. How do I be good enough to please you...to please you, Mom? How do I please your God? I want to do it right. Be it right.*

The trio finished and sat back on the pew. The woman strokes each boy's face and kisses each forehead. Both beam a smile into her gentleness. If they are staying for the 7:30 Mass they now have 20 minutes to wait in the quiet, on the pew of pain. The younger boy drapes his right arm over the back of the pew, and turns his body toward the rear of the sanctuary. He looks at me. I see him, and then I see past him. I see back. Way back through 63 years of space and time. I see *me* at seven, shortly after receiving my First

Holy Communion. *I was wearing THE white dress and veil every little Catholic girl anticipates. This was the best day of my seven year life. I felt clean and good and pretty. Mom was happy. I was bringing honor to the family. I was able to do what Mommy couldn't. She could not receive communion because she had committed the sin of divorce.*

Every Sunday, at the appointed time, Mom pushed her back against the pew, twisted her body as far to the side as she was able, making room for others to step over her as they made their way out into the aisle. Every week my mother watched others progress slowly to join the line of parishioners making its way to the altar. One by one everyone else made their way down the aisle to the altar and the priest, where they were given the "precious body and blood of our lord and savior Jesus Christ." He was the very same man who while here on earth taught the message of tolerance and forgiveness–loud and clear.

Today I think about the shame Mom must have swallowed, and my stomach tightens. All I understood as a seven-year-old on that day of my first holy communion, *Mom was happy, and I felt pretty and smart. I had learned the lessons and answered the questions. I never once drew an annoyed eye of attention from the priest or the nuns during the communion classes. I wasn't bad like some of the boys. I was perfect. It was a perfect day. We had dessert. I was sinless. But like the little boy sitting still on the pew in front of me, I got restless. I became bored. No one asked me questions. There was nothing to do but sit quietly.*

Somehow, quiet was the behavior God wanted. Sit still. No questions. No doubting. Sit quietly and do what you are told. The church will tell you what to think. And if you think about something we have told you not to think about, like kissing a boy, know that you have committed a sin. If you get angry or upset with your parents, or they with you, that behavior is also a sin upon your soul—a black mark. Only confession and constant vigilance can clean that black mark.

In Mexico, here I was again, restless in a Catholic church. A church and religion that no longer fit me. It doesn't fit my journey... just like my old corporate suits I sent to Goodwill when I slipped into my black yoga pants and began my private practice. Similar to when I decided to be self-employed, this religion does not fit me anymore. The judgmental God, the treatment of women, their rules for birth control, the clergy not allowed to marry... so much just doesn't fit.

I will forever be grateful for the quiet and peace the church offered me as a child. It was my safe place. I appreciate the way my Catholic education taught me to be charitable, to share with others and to respect ritual and mystery. And now, without any doubt, I know I am finished. There is nothing for me to gain by sitting on this pew of pain. My heart is finished with the theology. Again, I hear Bitch-babe (my critic), this time softer, more like an echo. *"You are so lame. You can't sit here and see what is revealed to you? You are not strong enough, Irene? Look what Jesus did for you! And you can't sit?"*

"No!" I reply. I am not sucked into your guilt. I don't buy your chatter anymore. I haven't for a very long time. But wow, I get how embedded you are in me. You are like using my right hand. I can't remember the day I started, and I know how hard it would be not to default to using it now. But no, not anymore, I am not doing your guilt.

I stood up and stepped out into the aisle. I turned my back to the altar and faced the open front doors. While I was inside, the sun had risen just high enough to see me from the other side of the world. It was laughing its warmth all over my face. I could see the barista at Starbucks turning the handles to open the table umbrellas. I crossed the threshold and walked through the open doors. Standing on the top step looking down onto the alley-way, now filled with early day activities, my heart was rich with gratitude for the sun and the life that greeted me.

I breathed in the light.

Enliven

Learning to give yourself experiences that enliven,
invigorate and lift you (No alcohol or drugs involved)

A note from David

It was a beautiful spring morning, Irene and I, coffee in hand, were sitting by our large picture window looking out onto the new green that was everywhere. We are early risers and like to start each morning with a spiritual reading. We follow many teachers...Thich Nhat Hanh, Pema Chodran, Lisa Natoli, Marianne Williamson, Wayne Dyer...so many wonderful teachers who have brought us wisdom and guidance. This has been our daily routine for years.

Irene said to me, "I'm having trouble writing about the fifth cairn." (**Do something that enlivens you every day.**) "What?" I said with amazement. "Irene, you are the epitome of enlivenment. That's why I married you. I can think of lots of ways we have enlivened our lives and you initiated most of them." She asked me if I would write them down. She wanted help with her epilogue. I barely lifted my pen when I filled a page of examples in my journal. Here are some of them... little things like walks, bike rides, reading a book out loud together, going out for lunch, taking the scenic way to a place rather than the fastest, stopping when the load of life just feels overwhelming and taking a dance break...literally putting on the music and dancing...taking a one-day vacation...driving up to the mountains to breathe in the new air and turning around the same day to drive home. Enlivening experiences are always about stopping and taking the time to be.

I read the list to her and she got it. She confessed she had been so wrapped up in writing this book that she was not living her own advice. She emphasized that she needed to stop, stop, stop, and breathe, breathe, breathe. She needed to breathe deeply and listen.

Enlivening happens when you give yourself any experience that changes the energy. Do something that forces you to put a bookmark in the demands of your day and say "yes" to the moment.

When you allow space, you open to the spirit of life that carries you forward. It is then you KNOW...there is more than you. You are not alone. You are part of a benevolent plan. Like no one else, Irene has been my teacher for this. I hope she has been that for you.

...closing thoughts...

Not a lot about aging is enviable. While I find most everything physical now presenting interesting challenges, the one saving grace through this getting-old process is an appreciation for my interior life. It proves to be exponentially richer by the day. I guess you must go inside when you are older because everything on the outside has turned on you. Lots of my body parts just don't respond like they used to, causing me to slow down. I enjoy stillness more often than ever in my life.

Throughout my life one of my strengths has been to find the blessing in whatever is happening. I wish I could find it faster, not so. But eventually I do find it.

The blessing from aging is I no longer hide from myself. I am no longer disconnected from my truth. In the quiet...in the stillness...there is me...and I can hear the voice of truth... the voice of God.

My prayer for you...

I wish you an open ear and heart to your inner guide. I pray for you that you learn to trust what you KNOW today. Don't wait another day to believe yourself. I pray that you always remember at your core you are the gold of creation. Life is showing up as you and through you.

Words from one of my favorite troubadours, David Roth...

Will you come home...
Will you come home...
Will you come home to your heart?
You've kept away from yourself from the start...
You can come home now...
Come home to your heart.

I wish you infinite blessings.
May you listen to your heart and know the love you are.
With much love and gratitude,

Blessings, Irene

There are so many authors who have guided my journey. These are some of my favorites for whom I am forever grateful...

Nancy Slonim Aronie–*Writing From the Heart*
Christina Baldwin–*Life's Companion–Journal Writing as a Spiritual Quest*
Mellody Beattie–*Co-dependent No More*
Julia Cameron–*The Artist's Way*
Pema Chodran–*Taking the Leap*
Dr. Wayne Dyer–*Your Erroneous Zones*
Louise Hay–*You Can Heal Your Life*
Richard and Mary-Alice Jafolla–*The Quest*
Dr. Jerold Jampolsky–*Love is Letting Go of Fear*
Anne Lamott–*Traveling Mercies*
Pia Mellody–*Facing Co-dependency*
Anita Moorjani–*Dying to Be Me...*
Lisa Natoli–*Gorgeous for God*
Dr. Scott Peck–*The Road Less Traveled*
Pat Rodegast and Judith Stanton–*The Emmanuel Series*
Marianne Williamson–*Return to Love*
Bill Wilson–*Alcoholics Anonymous*

Printed in the United States
By Bookmasters